SOFTWARE PROTOTYPING, FORMAL METHODS AND VDM

INTERNATIONAL COMPUTER SCIENCE SERIES

Consulting editors   **A D McGettrick**   University of Strathclyde

J van Leeuwen   University of Utrecht

SELECTED TITLES IN THE SERIES

SOFTWARE PROTOTYPING, FORMAL METHODS AND VDM

Sharam Hekmatpour
University of Melbourne

Darrel Ince
The Open University, Milton Keynes

ADDISON-WESLEY
PUBLISHING
COMPANY

Wokingham, England · Reading, Massachusetts · Menlo Park, California
New York · Don Mills, Ontario · Amsterdam · Bonn
Sydney · Singapore · Tokyo · Madrid · San Juan

The programs presented in this book have been included for their instructional value. They have been tested with care but are not guaranteed for any particular purpose. The publisher does not offer any warranties or representations, nor does it accept any liabilities with respect to the programs.

Many of the designations used by manufacturers and sellers to distinguish their products are claimed as trademarks. Addison-Wesley has made every attempt to supply trademark information about manufacturers and their products mentioned in this book. A list of the trademark designations and their owners appears on page x.

Cover designed by Crayon Design of Henley-on-Thames and printed by The Riverside Printing Co. (Reading) Ltd.
Printed in Great Britain by The Bath Press, Avon.

First printed 1988.

British Library Cataloguing in Publication Data
Hekmatpour, Sharam
  Software prototyping, formal methods and
  V.D.M. — (International computer science
  series).
  1. Computer systems. Software. Development.
  Prototyping
  I. Title II. Ince, D. (Darrel) III. Series
  005.1

  ISBN 0–201–17572–X

Library of Congress Cataloguing in Publication Data
Hekmatpour, S. (Sharam), 1961–
    Software prototyping, formal methods, and VDM/Sharam Hekmatpour
    and Darrel C. Ince.
        p.   cm. — (International computer science series)
    Bibliography: p.
    Includes index.
    ISBN 0–201–17572–X
    1. Computer software — Development.   I. Ince, D. (Darrel)
  II. Title. III. Series.
  QA76.76.D47H45 1988
  005.1′1—dc19   88-19400
                                                                              CIP

Preface

Just a few years ago, rapid prototyping was an alien subject to software developers. Today, there is hardly anyone in the software community who has not at least heard of the term. Having recognized the importance of the concept, an increasing number of software houses are now actively engaged in setting up working groups on prototyping, and most international conferences on software engineering and Human–Computer Interface are devoting entire sessions to the subject. Although general interest in this area has risen dramatically and research has been intensified, there is still a serious shortage of material on the subject as well as software tools to support it.

This book aims to alleviate some of these shortcomings. It first introduces the reader to rapid prototyping by examining the state of the art, and then describes a prototyping methodology based on formal methods of software development. The latter is supported by a wide-spectrum language, embedded in a UNIX-based prototyping environment called EPROS, which enables very rapid generation of working prototypes from a formal description of a system.

The book is intended for four classes of readers: researchers in software engineering, developers who use formal methods of software development, industrial staff who are looking for viable prototyping techniques, and university lecturers who are interested in using a software tool in their formal methods and prototyping courses. Apart from the first three chapters, which are of introductory nature, the rest of the book assumes that the reader is familiar with the Vienna Development Method (VDM) formal specification notation. No attempts have been made to teach VDM in detail, since there are already two excellent introductory books on the subject [Jones 1980a, Jones 1986]. We have also assumed that the reader is familiar with the notion of programming in general and a high level programming language like C or Pascal in particular.

The organization of this book is as follows. Chapter 1 provides some motivation and explains why prototyping is important. Chapter 2 discusses prototyping in more depth and provides a categorization of approaches to prototyping. Chapter 3 describes a number of prototyping techniques in some detail. Chapter 4 gives an overview of the EPROS prototyping system, its development procedure and the wide-spectrum language it is based on, and describes the available facilities in some detail. The use of the specification notation is illustrated by a case study in Chapter 6. Chapters 7, 8 and 9 describe the implementation, user interface development, and meta abstraction facilities of EPROS, respectively. The final chapter describes a second case study which puts the described techniques into practice. The last version of the prototype developed in this chapter may be found in Appendix B. Appendix A serves as a reference manual for EPROS, and describes the formal syntax of its notation, its libraries, and its command language.

S. Hekmatpour and D. Ince
June 1988

Acknowledgements

The authors and publishers would like to thank the following:

- Association for Computing Machinery for permission to quote from McCracken, D.D. and Jackson, M.A. 1982. 'Life cycle concept considered harmful,' *ACM SIGSOFT Software Engineering Notes*, 7(2) pp. 29–32.

- Elsevier Science Publishers for permission to quote from Bally, L., Brittan, J. and Wagner, K.H. 1977. 'A prototype approach to information system design and development,' *Information and Management*, 1 pp. 21–26.

- Oxford University Press for permission to reproduce material written by the authors and previously published in Zorkoczy, P.I. (ed.) 1986. 'Rapid software prototyping,' *Oxford Surveys in Information Technology*, 3 pp. 37–76.

A note on language
For reasons of simplicity, the pronoun 'he' is used to relate to both male and female throughout the book.

Contents

Chapter 1
Introduction

This chapter briefly describes some of the problems encountered with those conventional software development techniques associated with a phased software life cycle, and outlines how a prototyping approach is capable of overcoming these problems.

1.1 The life cycle model

For the past twenty years or so, software system development has been based on a model, commonly referred to as the software **life cycle** model [Zelkowitz *et al.* 1979, Boehm 1981, Sommerville 1982, Shooman 1982, Fox 1982]. Though characterized differently by different authors, its overall theme is well understood and universally acknowledged. The life cycle model leads to a software development strategy which is usually called the phase-oriented, the linear or the traditional strategy.

The life cycle model essentially advocates that software projects should consist of a number of distinct stages. These are: requirements analysis, requirements specification, design, implementation, validation, verification,

1

operation and maintenance. **Requirements analysis** is concerned with deriving, from the customer, the desired properties and capabilities of a proposed software system. **Requirements specification** involves stating the system functions and constraints in a precise and unambiguous way. **Design** is the task of producing, and consequently refining solutions that satisfy the specification. **Implementation** is the act of realizing the design in a programming language which can be executed on the target machine. **Validation** is the process of checking that a system fulfills its user requirements. **Verification** has the objective of ensuring that the end product of each of the first four stages matches its input. **Operation** is the activity of installing and running a completed system in its intended environment. Lastly, **maintenance** is the process of modifying a system, during its operational lifetime, to correct detected errors, improve performance, and incorporate newly emerging requirements.

The life cycle model was originally derived from the hardware production model of requirements, fabrication, test, operation and maintenance [Blum 1982]. It primarily reflects management concerns in production, such as planning, control, budget expenditure and resource allocation. Its aim is to provide a basis for estimating the correct distribution of labour and capital over a well planned period of time by dividing the production process into a number of rationalized phases, each with its own milestones and deliverables.

Central to the model is its linear structure; with exception of validation and verification, all other stages are carried out linearly, i.e., each stage begins only when the previous stage has been completed. The model works very well in hardware production; its appropriateness for software development, however, is becoming increasingly questionable.

1.2   Deficiencies of the life cycle

Software producers who currently use the life cycle model have to cope with three unpleasant facts: (i) the earlier an activity occurs in a project the poorer are the notations used for that activity, (ii) the earlier an activity occurs in a project the less we understand about the nature of that activity, and (iii) the earlier an error is made in a project the more catastrophic the effects of that error. For example, early requirements and specification errors have typically cost a hundred to a thousand times as much as those made during implementation [Boehm 1981], and have lead to a number of multi-million dollar projects being cancelled.

Increasing user dissatisfaction with software since the early nineteen seventies has motivated researchers to pay greater attention to the earlier stages of software development [Ramamoorthy *et al.* 1984]. As a result, many requirements analysis and specification techniques have been invented [Davis and Vick 1977, Ross and Schoman 1977, Taggart and Tharp 1977, Levene and Mullery 1982, Lehman and Yavneh 1985], some of which are even computerized [Smith and Knuth 1976, Teichroew and Hershey 1977, Bell *et al.* 1977]. At the same time there is a rapidly increasing interest in formal, more mathematical methods of software development which adherents claim lead to more reliable systems which have an increased probability of meeting user needs [Musser 1979, Davis 1979, Jones 1980b, Silverberg 1981].

Unfortunately, even when a software developer uses modern notations and techniques, success is likely only when the application is both well understood and supported by previous experience [Bally *et al.* 1977, Blum and Houghton 1982, Brittan 1980]. The current rate of growth in hardware has meant that each year large numbers of new applications emerge for which the old knowledge is inadequate. Faster and larger, cheaper memories mean that computers are being used in novel projects where the relation of the computer to its environment, to human operators, and to other computers has not been researched adequately. Many such projects are based on specifications which are not true reflections of the customer's requirements. This is due to three reasons.

First, there is usually a significant cultural gap between the customer and the developer and the way they communicate [Christensen and Kreplin 1984]. Consequently, a customer often finds it extremely hard to visualize a system by simply reading a technical system specification document [Gomaa and Scott 1981, Mayr *et al.* 1984]. If the customer is unable to visualize such a system then validation during the early part of the project becomes a very error prone activity. Indeed, the difficulties involved in communication with the user can be a serious barrier to proper development [McCracken and Jackson 1982]:

> 'The life cycle concept perpetuates our failure so far, as an industry, to
> build an effective bridge across the communication gap between end-
> user and system analyst. In many ways it constraints future thinking to
> fit the mold created in response to failures of the past.'

Second, the customer, unfamiliar with information technology, may have produced very vague requirements which could be interpreted arbitrarily by the developer [Brittan 1980]. Third, empirical evidence [Ackford 1967] suggests that once a user starts employing a computer system, many changes occur in his perception as to what the intended system should do; this obviously invalidates the original requirements. As a result, user requirements are often a moving target, and producing a system that meets them is a risky and error prone activity.

A further complication is that a software project of considerable size may take many years to complete; during this time the user requirements, as well as the user environment, may change considerably, making the final system even more obsolete [McLean 1976, Gladden 1982, Ramamoorthy *et al.* 1986]. This is graphically described by [Blum 1982]: 'Development is like talking to a distant star; by the time you receive the answer, you may have forgotten the question.'

The life cycle model is strongly based on the assumption that a complete, concise and consistent specification of a proposed system can be produced prior to design and implementation. The validity of this assumption has been challenged and refuted by a number of authors [Swartout and Balzer 1982, McCracken and

Jackson 1982, Shaw 1985]. In many cases a complete specification cannot be produced, simply because the user does not really know what he wants [Berrisford and Wetherbe 1979, Parnas and Clements 1986].

Lack of experience in projects where it is almost impossible to construct a precise specification leads to the situation where the customer requirements can be established only when a complete software system has been built and when the system can be examined in a fully concrete form [Blum and Houghton 1982]. For this reason many systems end up being written at least twice. To quote Brooks [1975]: 'Plan to throw one away; you will, anyhow.'

There are numerous examples in the literature of substantial modifications of systems during maintenance because of inadequate requirements analysis. For example, it has been reported [Boehm 1974] that in some large systems up to 95% of the code had had to be rewritten to meet user requirements. Even more formal, improved techniques and notations for requirements specification are not helpful in this respect, as the transition from the user conceptual model of a system to a specification of the system is an inherently informal process [Leibrandt and Schnupp 1984].

All evidence, therefore, suggests that the life cycle model has many shortcomings which may have adverse effects on software projects. This is, of course, not to say that this model should be rejected outright. To the contrary, in certain areas, such as embedded software and real time control systems, it is the most rational approach and indeed the best way of controlling the complexity of such projects. However, for the majority of other applications, especially those related to commercial data processing, it is inappropriate and has many deficiencies which are too serious to be ignored. The deficiencies may be summarized as follows.

- It is unable to cope with vague and incomplete user requirements [Brittan 1980, MacEwen 1982].

- It discourages feedback to the earlier stages because of the cost escalation problems [Bastani 1985].

- It cannot predict the effects of introducing a new system into an organization before the system is complete [Keen 1981].

- It cannot properly study and take into account the human factors involved in using the system.

- It introduces a computer system into an organization suddenly. This is a rather risky approach since users are known to resist significant, sudden social changes [Rzevski 1984].

- The customer may have to wait for a long time before actually having a system available to him for use. This could have undesirable effects on customer trust and may cause frustration [Gladden 1982].

- The final product will, at best, reflect the user requirements at the start of the project and not the end. In long projects, these two may differ considerably due to changes in the customer's organization and practices.

- Once the users start employing the final system and learn more about it, their views and intentions change significantly. Such changes in user perception can by no means be predicted [Clark *et al*. 1984].

1.3 The prototyping solution

In the light of the difficulties described above, many researchers have arrived at the conclusion that software development, particularly during its early stages, should be regarded as a *learning process* and practised as such [Mason and Carey 1983], and that it should actively involve both the developer *and* the customer [Christensen and Kreplin 1984]. For it to be efficient, it requires close cooperation, and can be successful only when it is based on an actual working system [Somogyi 1981]. Although customers are not very good at stating what they want from a future software system, they are very proficient at criticizing a current system!

A number of techniques have emerged in recent years that are based on this idea. They are classed under the generic term **rapid prototyping** [Smith 1982, Zelkowitz 1984]. The use of these techniques represents a major change in the way software is produced. They rely on an idea borrowed from other engineering disciplines – that of producing a cheap and simplified prototype version of a system rapidly and early in a project. This prototype becomes a learning device to be used by both the customer and the developer and provides essential feedback during the construction of a system specification. The prototyping approach, when compared to current methods, is so dynamic that the difference can be compared to that between interactive and batch oriented systems [Naumann and Jenkins 1982].

Like software testing [Meyer 1978], the main philosophical issue in prototyping is admission of failure; that we, as human beings, no matter how careful in our development practices, are likely to make mistakes. Bally *et al*. [1977] put the idea appropriately in the following words.

> 'In one sense the prototype strategy is an admission of failure, an admission that there will be circumstances in which, however good our techniques and tools for investigation, analysis and design, we shall not develop the right system at the first attempt. But surely this is only realism based on hard experience, theoretically ideal solutions are often far from satisfactory in a very imperfect world.'

One of the objectives of the prototyping approach is to reduce the maintenance effort. There is now considerable evidence [Swanson 1976, Zelkowitz *et al*. 1979, Lientz and Swanson 1980, Lientz 1983] that software maintenance can occupy between 50 to 90% of total project cost during the lifetime of a system. There is increasing empirical evidence [Boehm *et al*. 1984] that prototyping can indeed produce more maintainable products.

Overall, the limited results and experience which have been obtained have been very encouraging. For example, in a reported prototyping experiment [Boehm *et al.* 1984], systems were developed at 40% less cost and 45% less effort than conventional methods. Other researchers have reported even more impressive figures. Scott [1978] has described a system which was estimated to cost $350,000 to develop but was accomplished by a prototype that cost less than $35,000. The figures that have been reported have also supported the contention that prototyping shortens the overall development cycle for software [Berrisford and Wetherbe 1979, Mason and Carey 1983, Bonet and Kung 1984].

1.4   Summary

This chapter has only been introductory in nature. It has pointed out that there are a number of problems associated with conventional software development. Typical problems include the inability to cope with user requirements, and the late visibility of the software product. Software prototyping was presented as one solution to some of these very large problems and some empirical data was presented to support this.

Chapter 2
Rapid Software Prototyping

There are a number of misconceptions surrounding the topic of prototyping. This chapter aims to dispel them. The precise nature of prototyping is described, and the large number of applications of the technique outlined. One major misconception is that there is only one type of prototyping. There are, in fact, three: evolutionary prototyping, incremental prototyping and throw-it-away prototyping, and this chapter describes the features of each of these. The chapter continues with a description of the main prototyping activities, and then concludes with a discussion of both the benefits and disadvantages of adopting a prototyping approach.

2.1 What is prototyping?

Prototyping originated from those engineering disciplines which are involved in mass production. There, it refers to a well established phase in the production process whereby a model is built which exhibits all the intended properties of the final product. Such a model serves the purposes of experimentation and evaluation to guide further development and production. It is important to note that no kind of hardware production is conceivable without this phase.

In software engineering the notion of mass production is absent; instead, production refers to the entire process of building the one product. For this reason, the concept of prototyping takes a rather different meaning. Here, most commonly, it refers to the practice of building an early version of the system which does not necessarily reflect all the features of the final system, but rather those which are of interest. In particular, and in contrast to hardware production, we require a prototype to cost very little and to take a significantly short time to develop, hence the term **rapid prototyping**. The purpose, as before however, is to experiment, to learn and to guide further development.

As one would expect with any new term, there is some dispute over the exact meaning of prototyping within the context of software engineering. Some insist that it should be used to refer to a mocked-up initial version of a system which is thrown away after use [Gehani 1982a, Budde and Sylla 1984]. Others suggest that a prototype may become the final system by means of a process of continual improvement [Dodd 1980]. To avoid confusion, some authors suggest that the term prototype should be used to refer to the **throw-it-away** approach, and the term **evolutionary development** be used when a prototype 'evolves' to become the final system [Gilb 1981, Patton 1983].

Other terminologies exist. For example, throw-away prototypes have also been called **scale models** [Weiser 1982], although it has been argued [Dearnley and Mayhew 1983] that a model should be regarded as a pictorial representation whereas a prototype is a working system. It has also been suggested [Gregory 1984] that a system with a user interface similar to the final product, but incomplete in terms of functionality, should be called a **mock-up** and not a prototype. In contrast to this, the term **bread-board** has been suggested to refer to a system that has a high functionality and no user interface [Botting 1985].

Other relevant terms used in the literature are: test vehicle, engineering prototype and production prototype [Bally *et al.* 1977], heuristic development [Berrisford and Wetherbe 1979], infological simulation [Naumann 1982], system sculpture [Blum and Houghton 1982], iterative enhancement [Basili and Turner 1975], evolutionary development [Gilb 1981] and incremental development [Baldwin 1982].

It is not the intention of this book to discuss the merits of all these terms. For our purposes, however, we need to establish what we mean by a prototype. When referring to a prototype, we shall assume the following.

- It is a system that actually works; it is not just an idea or a drawing.
- It will not have a generalized lifetime. At the one end of the spectrum it may be thrown away immediately after use, and at the other end it may even become the final system.

- It may serve many different purposes, ranging from requirements analysis to taking the role of the final product.
- For whatever purpose, it must be built quickly and cheaply.
- It is an integral part of an iterative process which also includes modification and evaluation.

Throughout the rest of this book, by **prototype** we shall mean a rapid software prototype unless otherwise stated.

2.2 Applications of prototyping

Prototyping can be applied to various phases of the software life cycle and can also replace some or even all of them. In general, it can be applied to the following areas.

- To aid the task of analysing and specifying user requirements. Here it may have a complementary role, assisting the analyst in finding out actual user requirements. In some cases, the prototype itself may replace the requirements specification document.
- As a complementary tool in software design. For example, to study the feasibility and appropriateness of a system design, to verify novel designs, to contrast and compare the merits of alternative designs, and to demonstrate that a design meets its specification.
- As a tool to resolve uncertainty. For example, to study the effects of, and to cope with, organizational changes due to introduction of new technology, to gradually adapt a computer system to its intended environment, and to decrease the level of risk in introducing automation.
- As an experimental tool, to study the human factors of new computer systems, especially for deriving acceptable human-computer interfaces.
- As a vehicle to support user training in parallel to system development. This is one of the forgotten areas where prototyping would be useful.
- As an economic way of implementing one-shot applications [Smith 1982]. These concern problems which may be solved by writing a program and running it only once; after the solution is obtained the program will be of no further use.
- As a complementary tool in software maintenance, especially in situations where due to unstable user requirements heavy maintenance is expected, requiring much of the design to be re-worked.
- As a development method whereby the prototype evolves to the final system.

For many technical problems, however, prototyping is not a suitable solution. In such cases, prototyping is likely to have adverse effects, creating more problems than it actually solves. Examples are: space and time efficiency problems, error recovery problems, system security problems, concurrency problems (e.g., deadlocks), hardware interfacing problems, networking problems (e.g., congestion control) and heavy numerical calculations (e.g., solving partial differential equations).

In general, there are three major areas where prototyping, although possible, is not advisable:

- Embedded software.
- Real time control software.
- Scientific numerical software.

Interestingly enough, the life cycle model works rather well in these areas and there is usually no need for prototyping. One major area where prototyping could be most valuable is that which has dominated the software market: commercial data processing. The effectiveness of prototyping here has been demonstrated in many applications such as management information systems [Scott 1978, Read and Harmon 1981, Blum and Houghton 1982], decision support systems [Henderson and Ingraham 1982], business transaction systems [Dearnley and Mayhew 1981], database applications [Canning 1981], accounting systems [Earl 1978], language processors [Zelkowitz 1980, Kruchten and Schonberg 1984] and many others.

2.3   Categorizing prototyping

The question of whether a prototype should become the final system is an important one. Even if it is agreed that a prototype will become the final product, other questions, such as how it should be constructed and when it can be accepted as the final product, need to be answered. Because of the importance of the relationship between a prototype and the final system, a classification based on this criterion is appropriate. This is characterized by the following classification which divides the approaches to prototyping into three main categories.

2.3.1   Throw-it-away prototyping

This corresponds to the most appropriate use of the term prototype, and is often used for the purpose of requirements identification and clarification [Dearnley and Mayhew 1981, Kraushaar and Shirland 1985]. To stress the relevance of this approach to requirements analysis and specification, it has also been called

specification prototyping [Keus 1982] and **specification by example** [Christensen and Kreplin 1984].

The need for rapid development is the greatest for throw-away prototyping. Since the prototype is to be used for a limited period, quality factors such as efficiency, structure, maintainability, full error handling and documentation are of little relevance. The prototype may even be implemented on hardware or within an environment other than the one required for the target system. What is important about throw-away prototyping is the process itself and not the product [Floyd 1984]. The major part of the effort, therefore, should go into the critical evaluation of the prototype rather than its design.

The use of throw-away prototypes, however, is not limited to the specification phase. They may be equally useful in the design phase [Dearnley and Mayhew 1984, Bonet and Kung 1984]. Used in this way, prototypes are often a useful tool for exploring alternative designs and evaluating the appropriateness or feasibility of a new design idea. They are also useful in the testing of a developed system, where they can be used as a comparator that evaluates the correctness of the test results of the system [Weyuker 1982].

As throw-away prototypes can be easily employed within conventional projects, they do not require any major changes to current software development practices. The cost of throw-away prototyping is highly influenced by the availability of appropriate software tools. Very high level languages have been most commonly used [Zelkowitz 1980, Gomaa 1983].

2.3.2   Evolutionary prototyping

This approach is in complete contrast to throw-away prototyping [Blum 1983]; it is in complete antithesis to current software development methods. Proponents of this strategy argue that information systems, once installed, evolve steadily, invalidating their original requirements [Naumann and Jenkins 1982, Brittan 1980, Gilb 1981]. The purpose of the evolutionary approach is to introduce a system into an organization gradually, while allowing it to adapt to the inevitable changes that take place within the organization as a result of using the system [Rzevski 1984].

Evolutionary prototyping is by far the most powerful way of coping with change. This approach requires the system to be designed in such a way that it can cope with change *during* and *after* development. A design practice that does not take the possibility of change into account can lead to severe problems; this is illustrated by the following revealing remark [Alter 1980].

'Systems were strained badly or died as the result of corporative reorganization ... An old version of a planning model was abandoned as the result of a reorganization, only to have its basic logic restructured years later ... The conceptual design problem here is building systems that are truly flexible.'

In evolutionary prototyping a system grows and evolves gradually [Nosek 1984, Gilb 1985]. For this reason, the first prototype usually does not implement the whole application. Instead, enough development is carried out to enable the customer to carry out one or more tasks completely [Dyer 1980, Mittermeir 1982b]. Once more is known about these tasks and how they may affect other tasks, more parts of the system are designed, implemented and integrated with the existing components. This allows a continuous and gradual low risk development while the system is undergoing use.

Addition and modification are two essential features of evolutionary prototyping and result in new complete deliveries [Gilb 1981, Patton 1983]. Unlike the throw-away approach, the prototype is always installed and used at the customer's site [Rzevski 1984]. This is of prime importance as the use of a prototype within its actual application environment is the most effective way of performing a comprehensive task analysis.

The primary difference between this approach and conventional software development is that it is highly iterative and dynamic; during each iteration a re-specification, re-design, re-implementation and re-evaluation of the system takes place. As a result, the impact of early errors is far less serious. Furthermore, the initial version of the system is delivered very early in the project and throughout the development process an operational system is always available to the user. This not only supports user training alongside development but also ensures that the final system will not 'surprise' the users when eventually introduced [Hawgood 1982].

At some point in time the final prototype is eventually transformed into the final product. Depending on how well the system design has survived the evolution process the final prototype may serve as the production version or a complete redesign might be necessary to facilitate smoother maintenance. Once again, the availability of appropriate tools is vital. To cut down the redesign effort, a highly modular design which can cope with extension and contraction [Parnas 1972, Parnas 1979] should be employed. The success of the evolutionary approach is very much dependent on the ability of the designer to build flexibility and modifiability into the software from the start [Munson 1981].

2.3.3   Incremental prototyping

Here the system is built incrementally, one section at a time. Incremental and evolutionary prototyping have often been used as synonyms [Baldwin 1982, Dyer 1980]. However, there is a significant difference between the two. Incremental prototyping is based on one overall software design [Floyd 1984] whereas with evolutionary prototyping the design evolves continuously. In incremental prototyping a full scale design is first conducted and then modules are implemented and added in sequence. As with evolutionary prototyping the system grows gradually but in a considerably less dynamic way. Since the incremental approach mostly affects the implementation phase it can be used in conventional software projects [Blum 1986]. Consequently, it has also been called the *plug-in strategy* [Bally *et al.* 1977, Taggart and Tharp 1977]. Incremental prototyping provides less scope for adaptation than evolutionary prototyping but has the advantage of being easier to control and manage.

Prior to prototype development the nature of the prototype should be well-understood by both the customer *and* the developer, i.e., whether the prototype should be throw-away, evolutionary or incremental. This point has created considerable confusion in the literature. For example, it has been suggested that it is possible to decide on the nature of a prototype *after* it has been constructed and evaluated [McNurlin 1981]. This does not seem to be helpful as the design of a prototype is highly influenced by the developer's perception of what it should be used for. For example, because of the significant difference in their expected lifetime, the design of an evolutionary prototype is very different from that of a throw-away prototype [Patton 1983].

Some authors suggest that prototyping and conventional development methods are complementary rather than alternative approaches to system development [Riddle 1984, Iivari 1984]. This is certainly true in the case of the throw-away and incremental approach, but not the evolutionary approach.

2.4 Prototyping activities

To be effective, prototyping should be carried out within a systematic framework. The framework advocated here consists of four steps. These steps and the way they relate to each other are described below.

2.4.1 The establishment of prototyping objectives

It is essential to establish what a prototype is supposed to be used for and what aspects of a proposed system it should reflect. A clear statement of the lessons that are expected to be learned from the prototype is also required. This information should be recorded in a document for future reference.

2.4.2 Function selection

A prototype usually covers only those aspects of the system from which the required information may be obtained. The selection of the functions to be included in the prototype should be directly influenced by the prototype objectives. Depending on these objectives, prototyping may be carried out *horizontally*, *vertically* or *diagonally* [Floyd 1984, Mayr *et al.* 1984]. Horizontal prototyping involves including all the system functions in a prototype, where each function is considerably simplified and reduced. Vertical prototyping involves including only some of the functions, where each of these is fully realized. Diagonal prototyping is a hybrid of these two. Function selection often boils down to simplifying the original requirements to some extent. However, care should be taken to ensure that the assumed simplifications are both *consistent* and *continuous* [Rich and Waters 1982].

2.4.3   Prototype construction

Of great importance is the speed and cost of prototype construction. Fast, low-cost construction is normally achieved by ignoring the normal quality requirements for the final product unless, of course, these are in conflict with the objectives. Throughout construction it must be ensured that everyone is aware of the fact that the main purpose of the prototype is experimentation and learning rather than long-term use. Some of the most serious errors in prototyping have occurred when a customer assumes that a prototype is actually some form of a production system which can be used immediately.

2.4.4   Evaluation

This is the most important step in the prototyping process and must be planned carefully. The users of the system must have already been given proper training and resources should have been made available for evaluation sessions. During evaluation, inconsistencies and shortcomings in the developer's perception of the customer requirements are uncovered. Many features of the system may prove unexpected or inadequate to the user. As evaluation progresses, the customer learns more about the proposed system and his own needs. At the same time, the developer learns about the way the customer conceives the system. The prototype becomes an effective communication medium which enables the two parties to learn about each other, without requiring them to have an in-depth knowledge of each other's fields. The feedback obtained from the evaluation phase must be studied, recorded and used judiciously to improve the prototype.

The prototyping process usually involves a number of evaluation sessions [Naumann and Jenkins 1982]. After each session, the prototype is modified in the light of the experience gained from its use and then subjected to further evaluation. This process is carried out iteratively until the prototype meets the objectives. The time between the iterations is extremely important and must be planned carefully [Henderson and Ingraham 1982].

2.5   Benefits and difficulties of prototyping

The value of the prototyping approach and its suitability for use in software development may be assessed by comparing its advantages against the difficulties it may cause both to the developer and the customer. The advantages may be summarized as follows.

* Prototyping enables one to cope with fuzzy requirements [Bally *et al.* 1977].
* A prototype system may be used as a teaching environment. This facilitates user training alongside development. Also, users will not be frustrated while waiting for the target system [Gomaa and Scott 1981].
* A prototype facilitates effective communication between the developer and the user.
* Prototyping gives the user the opportunity to change his mind before committing himself to the final system [Groner *et al.* 1979].
* Prototyping enables the low-risk development of computer systems to be more feasible.
* Prototyping enables a computer system to be gradually introduced into an organization.
* Prototyping transforms the software development process into a learning process.
* Prototyping has the effect of increasing the chance that a system will be more maintainable and user-friendly [Somogyi 1981].
* Prototyping can reduce the cost and time of development [Dodd 1980, Naumann and Jenkins 1982].
* Prototyping encourages users to participate in the development process and improves their morale [Gill *et al.* 1982, Earl 1978].

Prototyping has also its pitfalls and difficulties; these are as follows.

* When carried out in an artificial environment which does not match the final user environment there is a chance that users could miss some of the shortcomings.
* The 'model effect' [Bally *et al.* 1977] or 'tunnel vision' [Sol 1984] might result in inappropriate conclusions being derived from a prototype.
* Iteration might not be easily accepted by software designers as it requires the discarding of their own work [Hawgood 1982].
* There is a danger that the prototyping process could converge to a set of requirements too quickly, missing some essential points [Henderson and Ingraham 1982].
* Resource planning and management can be difficult [Alavi 1984].

• It may be difficult to keep system documentation up-to-date.

Although there is an increasing body of evidence that prototyping has positive implications for the process of software development, a large part of the software community still remain sceptical. Prototyping is not accepted as readily as other engineering disciplines. One reason for this is that software education and training is still strongly based on the conventional model of software development. Another reason is that the prototyping approach still lacks a coherent methodology [Boehm and Standish 1983]. While the former can be solved by updating software courses, the latter can only be solved by further research. The ideas presented in this book is a step towards the latter.

2.6   Summary

This chapter has set the scene for the remainder of the book. It has described the rationale behind prototyping, and the reasons for adopting a prototyping approach. The three different types of prototyping have been introduced and the advantages and disadvantages of prototyping outlined.

Chapter 3
Techniques of Prototyping

In this chapter we describe a number of approaches to prototyping. These invariably aim to achieve the same goal — the quick and cheap construction of working prototypes — but vary in the way they go about doing this and the applications for which they may be suitable. A recent view of software development is that the processing and user interface of a system should be regarded as separate entities and designed as such [Draper and Norman 1985, Ten Hagen and Dresken 1985]. This view is adopted here by classifying the technical approaches to prototyping into those that are relevant to prototyping the functional aspects of a system and those that are relevant to user interface prototyping. However, this classification is not clean cut; some of the techniques are applicable to both categories.

3.1 Function prototyping

An important aspect of any computer system is its functional behaviour, i.e., what it must do. This is normally described by a functional requirements specification document, produced by either the developer or the customer. Waters [1979] provides a useful check list of technical facts that must be recorded in such a document. He uses this list to evaluate the completeness of a number of specification languages and concludes that none is even 40% complete. There is also empirical evidence [Bonet and Kung 1984] that once development progresses functional requirements may change and expand considerably. For example, in the case of the project reported in Bonet and Kung [1984], the requirements expanded by a factor of five, but were easily controlled by employing a prototyping approach. The importance of including the functional aspects of a system in a prototype, therefore, cannot be overstated. This section discusses some of the technical approaches to prototyping these aspects

3.1.1   Executable specifications

A promising approach to rapid prototyping is the executable specification approach [McGowan *et al.* 1985]. Here, the basic idea is that if a specification language is formal and has operational semantics then it is possible to construct a system that can execute it directly. One attraction of this approach is that it can eliminate the cost of producing a prototype altogether since the specification of a system has to be produced anyway.

Formal specification techniques can be broadly divided into two categories [Liskov and Zilles 1975, Claybrook 1982]. The first category is based on writing a specification as a set of *axioms* [Hoare and Wirth 1973, Guttag 1977, Furtado and Maibaum 1985]. Axioms may be written as algebraic equations which, when treated as rewrite rules, can specify the operational semantics of the specification. For example, an unbounded stack with three operations of NEW_STACK, PUSH and POP may be specified as

```
NEW_STACK:  → Stack
PUSH:       Stack, Element → Stack
POP:        Stack → (Element | Undefined)
POP(NEW_STACK()) = Undefined
POP(PUSH(stk,elem)) = stk
```

where the first three lines specify the syntax of operations and the last two lines specify their semantics as an axiom. This technique has been employed in the OBJ specification language [Goguen and Tardo 1979]. Systems now exist which can translate OBJ specifications into executable code. Similar ideas have been used in the language NPL, its successor HOPE [Burstall *et al.* 1980], and also in CLEAR [Burstall and Goguen 1981] and SPECINT [Darlington 1983]. Virtually all these languages allow the axioms to be written as conditional and pure equations [Drosten 1984].

The second category of formal specification techniques is the **abstract model** approach. This is based on specifying the functions of a system in terms of abstract mathematical objects such as sets and functions. The above stack problem, for example, can be specified in an abstract model-oriented method such as VDM as

```
Stack = Element-list
NEW_STACK: →
    post(stk,stk') ≙ stk' = <>
PUSH: Element →
    post(stk,elem,stk') ≙ stk' = <elem> ⌢ stk
POP: → Element
    pre(stk) ≙ stk ≠ <>
    post(stk,stk',res) ≙ stk' = tl stk ∧ res = hd stk
```

where a stack is modelled by a list and each operation is specified by predicates on its arguments, result, and the stack. Typical specification languages in this category are described in Jones [1980a], Silverberg [1981], Claybrook [1982], Sunshine *et al.* [1982], Morgan and Sufrin [1984], Beichter *et al.* [1984] and Berzins and Gray [1985]. Examples of related executable specification systems are described in Balzer *et al.* [1982], Farkas *et al.* [1982], Feather [1982a], Urban [1982], Henderson [1984], Belkhouche [1985], Kemmerer [1985], Lee and Sluizer [1985] and Zave [1986].

Henderson and Minkowitz [1986] provide a useful comparison of these two categories in the context of executable specifications. They conclude that the differences between these methods are more artificial than real, and illustrate how functional programming could form a suitable basis for both.

There are two potential difficulties in making a specification language executable. First, mathematical objects such as infinite sets cannot be represented in finite store and have to be restricted to finite representations. Second, very implicit constructs cannot be easily dealt with and often need to be replaced by more explicit constructs to facilitate execution. Although these problems have no simple solutions, they do not diminish the usefulness of executable specifications. Once a means of execution is available, the work involved in preparing a specification for execution is relatively small [Tavendale 1985].

Symbolic execution [Cheatham *et al.* 1979, Danenberg and Ernst 1982] has also been suggested as a means of both verifying and animating formal specifications. Symbolic execution is a term applied to the execution of programs in a form which produces algebraic rather than numeric values. For example, the fragment of a Pascal program

```
s:= 1;
for j:=1 to 5 do
    s:= s*a[j];
writeln(s);
```

will, when it is symbolically executed, produce the following product as an algebraic expression

a[1]*a[2]*a[3]*a[4]*a[5]

rather than a numerical product. This approach has the advantage of addressing the class of all possible implementations for a specification. Discussions of this type of execution to produce prototypes can be found in Guttag and Horning [1978], Cohen *et al.* [1982], and Feather [1982a]. Unfortunately, symbolic execution suffers from many problems that are only likely to be solved in the very long term. For example, the symbolic execution of anything but unrealistically small specifications produces an overwhelming amount of symbolic print-out. Consequently, it is unlikely that this technique will play any significant part in software prototyping in the near future.

To summarize, even though there are a number of difficult research problems outstanding, there are a number of advantages associated with prototyping by means of specification execution. Apart from being intellectually appealing, this technique ensures that a precise level of documentation is always available to the developer. A specification gradually evolves towards user requirements and, at each stage, a precise description of the system is available rather than being buried in a mocked up prototype. Another advantage is the low cost of producing a prototype; little extra work is normally required after a formal specification has been developed and validated.

3.1.2 Very high level languages

Very high level languages (VHLL) are programming languages in which it is possible to express complicated operations in a small amount of written program code [Podger 1979]. They can offer significant gains in increased productivity at the expense of inefficiency in terms of increased running time and storage needs. For this reason, they are valuable tools for prototyping. Some of the relevant features of VHLLs are as follows.

- They are interpretive and interactive; a user can interact with such languages in real time.

- They offer a rich set of objects together with numerous operations on these objects.

- The language notation is short and concise and usually very expressive.

- They are normally supported by powerful programming environments and debugging tools.

- Because of their extensive run-time checks, they are more productive than conventional languages.

One language that has been advocated for prototyping more than any other is APL [Tavolato and Vincena 1984]. The basic object in APL is the array and is supported by a large number of powerful operations. Most APL systems also provide flexible filing systems and a report formatting facility which makes them suitable for prototyping commercial data processing applications. Although APL programs are very concise, they can be quite cryptic and difficult to read. Thus, APL is only advisable for throw-away prototyping [McLean 1976]. A typical use of APL for producing a throw-away prototype for a large commercial system is reported in Gomaa and Scott [1981].

LISP [Wilensky 1984] is another VHLL that has been used for rapid prototyping (see for example Heitmeyer *et al.* [1982]). The language itself has a good reputation for very high productivity [Sandewall 1978]. Also, some very powerful programming environments have been built around LISP and, although primarily conceived as a language for artificial intelligence, it has a number of attractive features making it suitable for rapid prototyping.

PROLOG [Clocksin and Mellish 1984] has also been advocated as a rapid prototyping tool [Leibrandt and Schnupp 1984]. This language is representative of a recent development in programming techniques known as logic programming [Kowalski 1979] which employs a restricted form of logic to express an algorithm.

Currently PROLOG does not enjoy as much popularity as other VHLLs as a medium for prototyping. This is due partly to poor PROLOG programming environments [Venken and Bruynooghe 1984] and partly because PROLOG is still evolving and a number of important technical and language issues have remained unresolved. However, its underlying structure makes it a particularly useful current tool for prototyping database and expert system applications.

Two other VHLLs which have been used for prototyping are SETL and SNOBOL. SETL [Kennedy and Schwartz 1975, Levin 1983] is a programming language which is based on set theory. It has been used in prototyping the first approved compiler for the American Department of Defense language Ada [Kruchten and Schonberg 1984]. SNOBOL [Griswold *et al.* 1971] is a long-established programming language used for manipulating character strings; Zelkowitz [1980] reports on its use in prototyping a language processor.

VHLLs require rather large run time environments that can consume inordinate amounts of storage space. This makes them unsuitable for implementing a final product. They also tend to be many times slower than conventional high level languages. However, this does not diminish their utility for rapid prototyping as time and space considerations are often of little concern.

Being real time and highly interactive, VHLLs enable efficient experimentation with, and modification of, prototypes – almost a mandatory prerequisite for prototyping. However, no single VHLL is suitable for all prototyping tasks. Instead a choice should be made by considering which language is suitable for which application domain. For example, if the application in mind is an expert system then APL would be a poor choice while PROLOG or LISP would match the application domain more naturally.

3.1.3 Application oriented very high level languages

Application oriented very high level languages (AHLL) are languages that provide significant savings in implementation time by providing facilities concentrating on a specific application domain such as cost accounting or stock control [Martin 1982]. These languages are embodied by systems that are either interpretive or program-like. An interpretive system is one in which the user provides a description of an application and the system responds to user requests by performing the desired functions through interpreting the application description; such systems are often known as **application generators**. A program-like system is one in which the user provides a high level program-like description of an application and the system translates it into a program in a conventional programming language; such systems are often known as **program generators** [Luker and Burns 1986] and the language used is usually referred to as a **fourth generation language** [Read and Harmon 1981].

Application generators are highly parameterized and are used to model an application through adjustment of these parameters. The basic idea behind these systems is that if an application domain is well-understood then it is possible to provide systems that can cater for all possible (or at least the most common) functions that would be used in that application domain.

Prywes and Pnueli [1983] describe a program generator which is based on a non-procedural language [Leavenworth and Sammet 1974] called MODEL and is aimed at commercial data processing applications. A MODEL program simply consists of a description of data items and a set of equations which describe interrelations between the data items. This description is then translated into a PL/1 or COBOL program. The description is usually compact due to avoidance of input/output detail and the detailed processing that is to occur. Because of this, MODEL programs tend to be 5-10 times shorter than their equivalent COBOL or PL/1 programs. Furthermore, the comprehensive error checking available in MODEL is a major factor in increased productivity [Tseng *et al.* 1986]. The use of MODEL by an accountant, with limited computing background, to generate an accounting system is described in Cheng *et al.* [1984]. Another typical AHLL is HIBOL [Mittermeir 1982a]. It differs from MODEL, in that it is highly interactive. It allows the interactive definition of business forms and provides facilities for interfacing to a database.

By restricting themselves to small application domains, AHLL systems can achieve high efficiency. As a result, these systems have also been used for producing finished products. In addition, since they facilitate rapid development, they are able to support evolutionary prototyping. The use of such systems for this method of prototyping is detailed in Canning [1981]. This reports on the development of a system where the final product contained about 13 000 lines of code, most of which was produced by a program generator with the whole development process taking just six weeks.

An attractive advantage of AHLLs is that they can be used by staff with little computing experience. The major disadvantage of AHLL systems is their very limited scope. They are useful for such applications as accounting, payroll, and banking where the application domain is well understood and where there is a wealth of existing implementation history and expertise [Ramamoorthy *et al.* 1984].

3.1.4   Functional programming languages

Ever since its early days, computing has been dominated by procedural languages. Such languages allow the programmer to explicitly retrieve data from areas of store, carry out some operation such as addition or multiplication on the data, and then deposit it back into store again. Procedural languages such as FORTRAN and COBOL have dominated data processing since the nineteen fifties. However, a number of computer scientists have recently pointed out three serious drawbacks with such languages [Backus 1978, Stoy 1982]: they have become over-complicated, they are unsuitable for implementing software on the multi-processor machines that have been made possible by advances in very large scale integration technology, and programs expressed in such languages are mathematically intractable.

As a reaction against the disadvantages outlined above a new generation of functional programming languages [Henderson 1980, Darlington *et al.* 1982] have been designed. The impetus towards their development has been the emergence of new 'fifth generation' multi-processor architectures. Typical functional languages are SASL [Turner 1979], Miranda [Turner 1985], and ML [Gordon *et al.* 1979]. The prime attraction of these languages is their conciseness; functional programs tend to be much smaller and easier to develop than corresponding conventional programs. An example of the conciseness that can be achieved is shown below. It shows a Miranda program [Turner 1985] for taking a finite list of objects and returning the set of all permutations of the list. The corresponding procedural program, expressed in a language such as Pascal,would occupy at least ten lines of code.

```
perms [] = [[]]
perms x = {a:p | a<-x; p<-perms(x--[a])}
```

Functional programming languages are also a medium for a technique known as **transformational programming** [Darlington and Burstall 1976, Darlington 1981, Bird 1984, Barstow 1985]. This involves a developer producing an extremely concise program for an application which would be very inefficient in terms of memory space and processing time. This program would then be gradually transformed into a working system by the process of replacing inefficient parts by more efficient facilities of the functional language used. This obviously has important implications for evolutionary prototyping.

Functional programming languages are still in their infancy, and many research questions remain unresolved. Consequently, their scope as a prototyping tool has yet to be explored. However, given promised developments in fifth generation hardware technology over the next decade, functional programming should become an indispensable medium for prototyping.

3.1.5 The tool-set approach

Within the context of software prototyping a tool can be defined as a program that aids the rapid construction of a prototype system. A prototyping tool-set is an environment offering a collection of such tools and a support facility for combining and integrating them quickly and easily.

The most well known tool-set is the UNIX operating system [Bourne 1983]. Although it was not originally designed for the purpose of prototyping, UNIX offers features that make it suitable for this purpose. The UNIX approach is based on providing a large number of tools [Bell Laboratory 1979] that include various language processors, analyzer generators, filters, report formatters and many others. The most significant feature of the UNIX tool-set is a uniform and clean common interface. The common interface is called **pipe** and allows the output of one tool to be passed to the input of another tool. Furthermore, the more sophisticated tools, such as LEX and YACC which can quickly generate language processors, have all been interfaced to a common programming language (C).

Prototyping in UNIX often means breaking a problem down into a number of steps where each step is realized by a tool [Kernighan 1984]. The tools are usually applied successively to data so that the output from one tool becomes the input to another. The high level control which determines the flow of data is obtained through a program known as the *shell* which is a programming language in its own right. In UNIX, the shell acts as glue, joining the tools together with minimal effort. To give an example, consider a program which processes a file of employees, where each employee is represented by a record consisting of his or her name, salary, etc., and produces a sorted file of those employees earning more than £10,000. It may be implemented as the following shell procedure.

```
cat employees | awk'$2 >= 10000'| sort +0 -1>high_earnings
```

Here the vertical bars are pipes and > writes the output to a file. A number of projects which have used the UNIX tool-set approach are discussed in Gehani [1982a] and Gray and Kilgour [1985].

Van Hoeve and Engmann [1984] describe another tool-set called TUBA which is specifically designed for the rapid prototyping and development of business application programs. TUBA is built around the programming language Simula-67 [Birtwistle *et al.* 1973]. It provides facilities for screen formatting and for this purpose it uses a data dictionary to store the pictorial description of objects manipulated and displayed by the system.

3.1.6 Reusable software

The relevance of reusable software [Horowitz and Munson 1984] to rapid prototyping is obvious. If a number of useful modules are available then it is possible to produce a crude, but rapidly constructed version of a system by joining these modules together. Since the emphasis in prototyping is on ease and speed of construction, reusable modules must have some specific properties. First, and most important of all, they must all have a simple and clear interface [Kernighan and Ritchie 1978, Meyer 1982]. Second, they should be highly self-contained, i.e., they should not be dependent on any other module or data structure as far as possible [Parnas 1972, Hall 1986]. Third, they must provide some very general functions [Polster 1986]. Good documentation is, of course, vital. An absolutely minimal documentation standard would insist on a description of each module's interface, function and error conditions.

Reusing old modules is not a new technique; it has been practised in certain application areas for a very long time. These modules are usually provided in pre-compiled form in a library. The widely-known Numerical Algorithms Group (NAG) library of general-purpose numerical analysis subroutines is a good example. The domain of applications that have used reusable modules has been very limited. The reason is that very few good general-purpose libraries exist. However, the high cost of software development is now providing an impetus to research in this area. This research has included the use of very high level programming languages [Cheng et al. 1984], the use of a functional programming language to control libraries written in Ada [Goguen 1984], and the transformation of programs written in one language to another language [Boyle and Muralidharan 1984] or to the same language [Cheatham 1984]. Recent practical experiences with developing systems from reusable software are reported in Lanergan and Grasso [1984], Matsumoto [1984], Litvintchouk and Matsumoto [1984] and Polster [1986].

Since applications vary considerably from developer to developer, it seems reasonable to suggest that each developer should put serious effort into collecting reusable modules [Neighbours 1984], even though the tight requirements for reusable modules may require a change in a developer's design practice. However, this change should not conflict with good design practices and is, in fact, a strong pre-requisite for good design. A number of criteria for decomposing systems into modules have been advanced [Parnas 1972, Parnas et al. 1985]. Much stress is placed on the importance of information hiding and that the design process should start with considering difficult design decisions, especially those that are likely to change with time. Each such decision is then hidden by means of a module. As Parnas demonstrates, this not only results in a clear design but also produces a set of highly independent, cohesive modules where each has a well-defined function and with minimal connection to other modules.

Although program code has normally been the medium for writing reusable modules, the ideal medium is a software design notation [Kant and Barstow 1981]. The most serious problems that have occurred in employing reusable software have been connected with implementation and programming language details [Balzer *et al.* 1983]. A machine-independent software design which has been precisely documented does not suffer from such problems and can normally be implemented quickly on a wide variety of computers and in different languages.

3.2   User interface prototyping

In current interactive systems a large part of the system is devoted to managing human–computer interaction. Sutton and Sprague [1978] report that, on average, about 60% of the program code accounts for the user interface. It should not therefore be surprising that a major part of a software project effort may be expended on the design and implementation of the interface.

User interface design is an inherently difficult task. There are a number of reasons for this. Specifying a user interface can be very difficult. Written specifications are even less helpful when compared to their use in specifying functionality. There is always a definite need to be able to visualize the appearance of a system [Lenorovitz and Ramsey 1977] and this is exactly where written specifications fail. A single system may have a variety of users with considerably different backgrounds [Van Meurs and Cardozo 1977, Carey 1982, Kruesi 1983]. Attempting to design an interface which is appealing to all users is not a simple task. The complexity of the requirements for a user interface often results in conflicting design goals which necessitate a compromise [Shneiderman 1979]. It is difficult to detect conflicts on the basis of paper studies and even more difficult to reach a suitable compromise. Desirable properties of a user interface such as user friendliness and ease of use are highly subjective and are revealed only when a system becomes operational [Tomeski and Lazarus 1975]. The traditional methods of software development have been relatively unsuccessful in the design of human–computer interfaces for the following reasons.

- Usually a user interface is not thought of in advance, or not even designed [Mills 1985]. Most design decisions are left unclear, giving the designer the freedom to decide how the user interface should operate. The designer constructs the interface around his own conceptual model which, in most cases, is distant from a user's conceptual model [Hayes *et al.* 1981, Dagwell and Weber 1983].

- The issue of user acceptability [Young 1981, Foley and Van Dam 1982] is not dealt with adequately; this inevitably leads to systems which are hard to use.

- The user interface is a major part of the system and is subject to continuous change more than any other part [Munson 1981]. The need for change is rarely thought of in advance.

- It is now well recognized that the user interface should be designed as a separate entity from the rest of a system [Edmonds 1981, Green 1985]. This not only eases maintenance but also simplifies the task of providing a number of interfaces to the same system. This advice is rarely followed. Those parts of the system responsible for human–computer interaction are usually embedded so deeply in the system that their modification requires changes on a global scale.

Proper design of the user interface is such an important step in system development that many authors believe that it should be the first part of the system to be designed [Ten Hagen 1980]. The high degree of uncertainty and the possibility of change are good reasons why the design of a user interface should be carried out in an experimental and adaptive manner [Edmonds 1982] and why it should always consider the user model as an important issue [Green 1981, Norman 1983, Draper and Norman 1985]. Unfortunately, the design of such interfaces still remains more an art than a science [Smith *et al.* 1982, Turoff *et al.* 1982]. There are no well-understood procedures that can be followed to guarantee a successful design. Much of what is known is in the form of guidelines [James 1980, Gaines 1981]. An obvious problem with using such guidelines is that they are unmeasurable and subjective [Shneiderman 1979].

The prototyping approach recognizes the above difficulties by requiring the design of a user interface to be an iterative process involving a large degree of user participation. This approach allows the designer to derive a conceptual model that is appealing to a majority of users. Actual design of the system only starts when a reliable conceptual model is discovered. There are a number of technical approaches which can be used for prototyping the user interface. They are discussed below.

3.2.1 Simulation

One promising approach to the design of a human–computer interface is that of simulation [Clark 1981]. It is a powerful means of studying both user behaviour and the effectiveness of a proposed system, especially when little experience exists of the technology to be used in constructing the interface [Meijer 1979]. Simulation is very effective when the problem area is ill-structured [Bosman and Sol 1981].

An interesting use of simulation is outlined in Gould *et al.* [1983]. It describes an experiment in which users were exposed to a 'listening typewriter'. The study was carried out by having an operator and a user in separate rooms each equipped with a VDU terminal. The user would compose his letters by speaking through a microphone. User requests would be intercepted by the operator who would carry them out accordingly, thus giving the impression that the computer was in control. The aim of the study was to compare the user's performance and reactions to a listening typewriter as compared with the conventional means of composing letters. The use of simulation allowed the authors to study aspects such as speech mode, size of vocabulary, composition strategy and user experience. Most important of all, it enabled them to decide whether an imperfect listening typewriter would be of any utility. This study is important in the sense that it demonstrated that human factors can be studied very effectively through a simple and cheap simulation exercise prior to costly development.

When carrying out a simulation the first task is to derive a simple model of the real system to be developed. This model forms a vehicle for conducting experiments that would otherwise have to be carried out on the real system. The purpose of simulation is to gain insight into the behaviour of a system and also to evaluate techniques behind the operation of a system [Shannon 1975]. Simulation is a methodology for problem solving and is most effective when the real world experiments are too costly and impractical to perform. Some authors consider prototyping as a specific instance of simulation [Sol 1984].

3.2.2   Formal grammars

Formal grammars are a useful mathematical tool for the specification and design of human–computer interaction. These are notations used to describe the syntactic structure of various languages. The most commonly used notation is the Backus-Naur Form (BNF) which was originally designed for the specification of the syntax of programming languages [Naur *et al.* 1963].

The specification of a human–computer dialogue consists of two parts: the first part is the specification of the user input; the second part is the specification of the system's response to that input. Using BNF, one can easily specify user input formally and concisely [Shneiderman 1982]. The specification of a system's response to user input is not possible without extensions to BNF. Such an extension will introduce semantic actions into a BNF description. These actions check the validity of the user input and perform the required requests. For example, a simple mailing system with a single command for sending documents to users may be specified as

```
<mail> ::= 'send' document 'to' user[send_mail($name1,$name2)]
<document> ::= {'A'..'Z'}+ [$name1 = match]
<user> ::= {'A'..'Z'}+ [$name2 = match]
```

where the parts enclosed in square brackets represent the semantic actions. This approach has been used in a tool which takes a BNF description of graphical input devices and produces a prototype user interface [Hanau and Lenorovitz 1980].

If the user interface is based on a simple command language then compiler generator tools can be used to prototype the user interface. Such tools have, in the past, enabled developers to rapidly produce translators for programming languages from a BNF description of a language. One such tool which has proved useful in user interface design is the UNIX-based YACC compiler generator [Johnson 1975].

A different and more ambitious approach to the use of formal grammars for dialogue design involves what is known as the command language grammar (CLG) [Moran 1981] which describes a user interface at four levels; these being the task, the semantic, the syntactic and the interaction levels. CLG, although important as an attempt to extend the use of formal grammars, does not seem to be immediately suitable for prototyping purposes. It produces very long and detailed specifications that are often too complicated to comprehend. Furthermore, no automated tools are available to support its use. CLG, however, is a useful conceptual framework for the specification and design of dialogue systems [Davis 1983, Browne 1986].

An interesting use of formal grammars for prototyping has been suggested by Reisner [1981] who used formal grammars as a predictive tool to make a pre-development comparison of alternative designs. She predicted that certain properties of the BNF description of a user interface determine the complexity of the interface. To substantiate her claims she performed an experiment that demonstrated the correlation of empirical results of user performance with her predictions. Two similar approaches to user interface evaluation using formal grammars are described in Blesser and Foley [1982] and Wang [1970].

Formal grammars are by no means the ideal tool for dialogue design and prototyping. They have a number of problems [Jacob 1983]. For any serious dialogue, the BNF description can become very complicated and incomprehensible. As a result, it may be very difficult to decide what event might occur after a series of user actions and vice versa. BNF is also particularly weak in describing error cases and help messages. Such messages must occur at very specific points in the dialogue and their inclusion often requires adding further complicated rules to a BNF description which do not seem to correspond to any reasonable concept.

3.2.3   State transition diagrams

The use of state transition diagrams (STD) for dialogue specification and design was first proposed by Parnas [1969]. The concept has also been used for specifying the functional requirements of computer systems [Casey and Dasarathy 1982].

An STD is a directed graph consisting of nodes and edges. Each node is usually represented by a circle and denotes a state of the dialogue. Nodes are connected by edges representing transitions between states. With each edge an input stream may be associated indicating that a transition between states will occur if the user input matches the specified input stream. STDs of this type have been used in the design of lexical analysers, parsers and compiler generators [Conway 1963, Johnson 1968]. Like formal grammars, in order to be useful for dialogue design, some extensions to the STD notation are necessary. Two extensions are usually provided [Casey and Dasarathy 1982, Kieras and Polson 1983, Wasserman 1985]. The first extension allows each edge to be labelled with an output message. This message is sent to the user when the associated transition takes place. The second extension incorporates semantic actions into an STD. These actions are again associated with edges and are invoked by transitions. For example, the mailing system described in the previous section can be specified by the following STD, where a slash is used as a separator between user input and corresponding computer action.

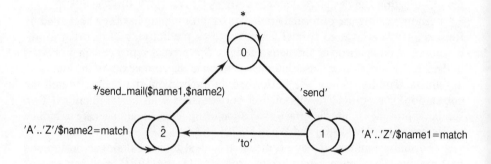

A number of tools have been constructed that convert an STD specification of a user interface into a prototype of the user interface [Wasserman and Stinson 1979, Wasserman and Shewmake 1982a, Wasserman and Shewmake 1982b, Jacob 1983]. In all these tools a linear textual notation is used for specifying STDs. The tools process the specification of a command driven user interface expressed in this notation, and immediately generate a finite state automaton which is a prototype user interface.

An important characteristic of STDs is that they make the state of a dialogue explicit and hence more readable; with formal grammars, this information is always hidden and usually very difficult to extract. This feature of STDs is very important from the point of view of the staff carrying out prototyping [Norman 1983]. An STD specification is also an exceptionally useful aid in the design of error/help facilities [Feycock 1977]. In an interesting study [Guest 1982] two dialogue design systems were compared. One system, SYNICS [Edmonds and Guest 1984], used the formal grammar approach while the other was based on state transition diagrams. SYNICS was rejected by almost all the staff who used it; the reaction to the other system, was positive and was used productively by non-computer staff.

3.2.4   Other formal methods

There are a number of other formal methods which have been applied to the specification and, in some cases, prototyping of user interfaces. One approach reported in Hopgood and Duce [1980] uses production systems as a basis for specifying human–computer interaction. Production systems are extensively used in expert systems and are based on situation-action or if–then rules [Winston and Horn 1981]. The use of production systems in dialogue design involves producing a knowledge base of if–then rules, where each rule associates a predicate over user input (and possibly systems states) to a system action in response to that input.

Although similar in some sense to state transition diagrams, production systems are distinguished by the fact that they avoid specifying input/output order. Interesting enough however, an STD can always be mapped to an equivalent production system easily.

Formal functional specification notations have also been applied to dialogue specification. Examples of these are given in Feather [1982b], Sufrin [1982, 1986], Cook [1986] and Meandzija [1986]. Chi [1985] provides an interesting evaluation of the use of four formal notations for dialogue specification which includes both algebraic and model oriented methods. He demonstrates that, while these notations are capable of specifying interaction, their use is difficult and time consuming. This is not surprising, as these notations were not originally invented for the purpose of dialogue specification, and fall short of many useful dialogue oriented features. Indeed, what they lack most is a suitable underlying model for specifying interaction.

One such model is described in Alexander [1986] and is an extension to a current formal specification and prototyping notation called ME-TOO [Henderson and Minkowitz 1986]. This model is based on the notions of dialogue events and finite state machines, and uses a LISP-like read-eval-print concept to model interaction. Another method is described in Silbert *et al.* [1986] and is based on the object oriented programming paradigm. In this model a user interface is designed as a network of objects of predefined classes which depict different views of the dialogue and which communicate to one another by passing messages. The model is primarily intended for graphical user interfaces but is general enough to be applicable to other applications as well.

3.2.5   Screen generators and tools

The appearance of the screen display is usually of great importance to a user. The traditional methods of screen design usually rely on producing paper drawings of screens. There are two difficulties with this approach: the drawings can take considerable time and effort to produce, and experience has shown that what seems to be acceptable on paper appears very different when displayed on a VDU screen. Software developers now recognize that the best way to reach an agreement on screen layout is by actually producing them on a VDU and carrying out a repeated process of modification until the user agrees with the presentation. However, programming such screen displays is a time consuming and expensive task and can only be economically carried out by means of prototyping tools.

Screen prototyping tools fall into two categories. The first category is based on providing a high level notation for screen definition. This is implemented either by means of a processor which converts screen definitions to a prototype version of the screen display [Christensen and Kreplin 1984], or as a package of library routines accessible from a programming language [Dixon 1985, Sale 1985, Kenneth 1981].

The second category makes use of sophisticated screen editors to produce the screen layouts interactively [Mittermeir 1982a], where each time a screen is produced it can be stored in a database and subsequently re-displayed. Both approaches allow rapid generation of a *scenario* of the application user interface. A scenario is a way of presenting to the user the sequence of events he or she would experience while performing some task and is more concerned with the presentation than the actual processing behind it.

The use of scenarios for the design of interactive systems has been advocated as the most eloquent way to design a human—computer interface [Hooper and Hsia 1982, Mason and Carey 1983]. Scenarios usually contain little or no application logic, so the sequence of events occurs in a predetermined, fixed order. This, nevertheless, is a very useful concept which allows the user to experience a system prototype without the developer committing many human and computer resources to implementation.

Mason and Carey [1983] have employed these ideas in a systematic way. They have devised a technique known as the **architecture-based** methodology. It takes its name from the similarity of the approach to the way buildings are developed: the technique places great importance on the external view of a system. The designer starts with an external view of the system and works inward from this. During this process the designer has the responsibility of ensuring that the system appearance is both acceptable and understandable to the user. The methodology is supported by a tool called ACT/1 which rapidly produces scenario prototypes of systems.

In a way, the architecture-based methodology is the reverse of conventional approaches to system development where the system grows from the inside outward, with its appearance becoming known only when it is fully constructed. The most significant advantage of this methodology is that it ensures that the system appearance is acceptable to the user during the whole of the development process. A limitation of this methodology is that it is only suitable for producing interactive information systems. In these systems the user interface dominates the entire system and its quality accounts for the quality of the system as a whole.

The architecture-based approach is representative of a number of recent approaches which argue that system development should start with the user interface. Other approaches to aid the construction of interfaces are described in Buxton *et al.* [1983], Aaram [1984] and Van Hoeve and Engmann [1984].

3.2.6   Language supported facilities

Another way of prototyping user interfaces is via facilities built into a programming language [Shaw *et al.* 1983]. These facilities have the potential of eliminating the need for dealing with the very low level detail commonly found in programming human–computer interfaces.

Almost all current programming languages were designed with an emphasis on batch processing rather than interactive computing [Shaw *et al.* 1983]. This is evident from the type of input/output facilities provided by them; these facilities are usually limited to reading and displaying strings and numbers. Modern interactive systems rely on much more flexible and powerful concepts of interaction (e.g., windows) [Ten Hagen and Dresken 1985]. Therefore, it is not surprising that much of the design and programming effort in user interface construction is expended on implementing these facilities by employing painstaking, laborious and error prone low level programming. Early work in this area has been centred around very high level languages. Examples include the use of LISP for prototyping command languages [Levine 1980] and the report generation facilities of APL [Tavolato and Vincena 1984].

There are four types of facilities which are increasingly being used in modern interactive systems; these are electronic forms, menus, overlapping windows and icons. Suitable extensions to programming languages would allow the use of these facilities to be specified rather than programmed using procedural facilities [Van Wyk 1982, Mallgren 1982].

The specification and design of electronic forms using language supported facilities is extensively described in Gehani [1982b, 1983], Yao *et al.* [1984] and Tsichritzis [1982]. Language facilities for specifying and prototyping icons and menus are discussed in Brown [1982], Gittins *et al.* [1984] and Lafuente and Gries [1978]. The use of windows is detailed in Teitelman [1979] and Rowe and Shoens [1983]. The provision of programming language constructs to support abstract input/output tools is discussed in Bos [1978] and Bos *et al.* [1983].

An alternative approach to supporting modern interaction concepts via a programming language is to use a **tool-box**. A tool-box is a coherent collection of interaction facilities built around a hardware architecture. The best designed tool-box of this kind is probably that of the Apple Macintosh [Apple 1985]. This has an object oriented design and is extremely well documented. Although tool-boxes as such are very flexible (and usually very efficient) they are hardware dependent. In many cases prohibitively so.

3.3   Discussion

It would be useful to compare the techniques described above in terms of their potential application domains and usefulness. This is summarized in Table 3.1 which summarizes much of what has been written in this chapter.

Table 3.1   A comparison of prototyping techniques.

Technique	Domain	Advantage	Disadvantage
executable specs.	functionality	concise & productive	not all specs. are executable
VHLL	language-dependent	productive	often cryptic
AHLL	very restricted	very productive	very application dependent
functional PL	functionality	concise	often inflexible
tool-sets	tool dependent	very productive	incoherent
reusable software	general	very productive	initially expensive
simulation	general	early application	no general support tools
formal grammars	certain interactions	concise	inflexible
STD	interaction	graphical	textual notation often cryptic
screen generators	mostly static dialogues	productive	inflexible
language facilities	language-dependent	concise & productive	restricted utility

Examination of this table leads us to the conclusion that none of the techniques can, on its own, be regarded as a complete and comprehensive prototyping tool. Each technique, while capable of capturing some aspects of an application, falls short of being applicable to others. Even the ones which have been classified as general have their own problems. In the reusable software approach, for example, no matter how many reusable modules we have at our disposal, moving to a new application will always require the development of additional unforeseen modules.

Previous researchers have concentrated on devising systems that each support only one of the above techniques (see for example Goguen and Tardo [1984],

Jacob [1983], Mason and Carey [1983], Prywes and Pnueli [1983], Shaw *et al.* [1983], Cheng *et al.* [1984] and Turner [1985]). This in turn has limited the utility of such systems for prototyping. The incompleteness of individual techniques and their highly different properties suggest that a *combination* of some of these techniques may be required in order to produce a powerful and general prototyping tool.

The next chapter will describe the combination of techniques that we have adopted and a system that implements and integrates these techniques within a coherent framework. The combination may seem rather arbitrary and is obviously one of many possibilities. We shall show, however, that it is an effective one and that it can accommodate all prototyping approaches described previously.

3.4 Summary

There are a number of categories of prototyping and, within each category, a number of techniques. This chapter has described these techniques. The major point that emerges from this chapter is the wide variety of tools, methods and techniques that are available for the prototyper. The chapter concludes with a comparison of these tools, methods and techniques.

Chapter 4
The EPROS Prototyping System

In this chapter we give an overview of our approach to prototyping and its application to system development. The approach and its methodology are supported by a development and prototyping environment called EPROS. In EPROS a system is developed in a top-down manner, from the abstract to the detailed. Progress is iterative and cyclic, where each cycle produces a self-contained description of the system. This description, no matter how abstract or how detailed, is always executable and is automatically converted into a working prototype.

4.1 The approach and its scope

The EPROS approach is based on utilizing and integrating four technical approaches to prototyping (see Chapter 3); these are:

- Executable specifications
- State transition diagrams
- Language supported facilities
- Reusable software

The functional requirements of a system are formally specified in META-IV [Jones 1980a, Jones 1986]. EPROS automatically translates such specifications into working prototypes. The user interface of a system is formally specified using state transition diagrams [Denert 1977]. EPROS provides an executable textual notation for describing these diagrams. User interface development and prototyping is further backed up by language supported facilities which have been especially designed to simplify the task of constructing user interfaces. Language supported facilities can be readily extended by the programmer through a facility called cluster which is also the main tool for reusable software development.

EPROS supports the three main approaches to prototyping: the throw-away, the incremental and the evolutionary approach. When used for throw-away prototyping, a system is first formally specified and then automatically converted into a prototype. Next, the prototype is evaluated by the user, whose feedback is used to improve the prototype. Any changes to the prototype are carried out by modifying the specification and regenerating a new prototype. This process is repeated until the prototype converges to a stable set of user requirements, at which time the prototype is discarded and the final system description is used for initiating a separate development process.

When used for incremental prototyping, an overall specification of the system is first produced (possibly using the throw-away approach). This specification is refined to generate a design which is then frozen. A small subset of the design is selected as the first increment; this is fully developed and handed over to the customer. The rest of the design is broken down into subsequent increments which are developed similarly and handed over to the customer one by one. User feedback obtained during this process is used to improve the increments. The architecture of the system, however, will remain intact; any requested changes will be restricted to the implementation of the increments.

EPROS is primarily intended to be used for the evolutionary approach. Evolutionary prototyping has three important requirements: fast iterations, intermediate deliveries, and gradual evolution of prototypes towards the final product. The executable specification features of the system cope with the first two requirements. The system also provides extensive facilities for the design and implementation of software systems; these support the last requirement of the evolutionary approach. Because of this comprehensive support, the entire development takes place within the system and is expressed in one notation, i.e., EPROL (see Section 4.3).

EPROS relies on the use of formal methods and notations for two reasons. The first reason is the potential of these methods for the automatic and fast generation of prototypes. The second reason is the power of these methods in producing clear and flexible designs [Jones 1977, Musser 1979, Feather 1982b, Sufrin 1982, Morgan and Sufrin 1984, Berzins and Gray 1985, Minkowitz and Henderson 1986, Weber and Ehrig 1986].This is highly crucial and indispensable for evolutionary prototyping, since, without a good design, modifications and extensions become totally impractical. The Vienna Development Method (VDM) was chosen as the underlying formal method since it is a well-developed methodology and has been used successfully in the development of many non-trivial systems [Hansal 1976, Cottam 1984, Minkowitz and Henderson 1986, Bloomfield and Froome 1986] (see Section 5.1).

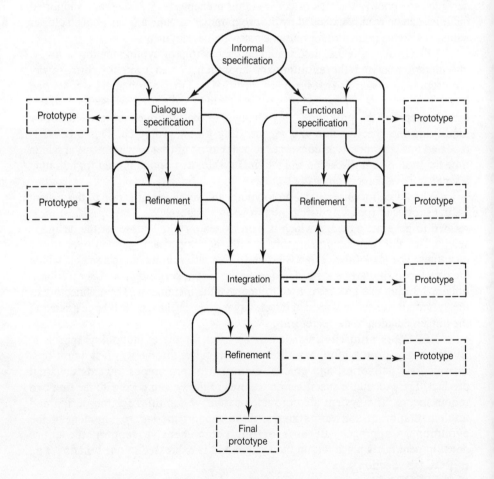

Figure 4.1 The evolutionary prototyping procedure of EPROS.

THE EPROS PROTOTYPING SYSTEM 39

4.2 The development procedure

Figure 4.1 shows a schematic view of the evolutionary prototyping procedure of EPROS. Development always starts with an informal specification of user requirements, which may be vague, incomplete and unstable. After a preliminary study of the requirements a formal specification is produced. The first specification may consider only functional requirements, or only those related to the user interface, or both. Usually, however, one starts with the functional requirements, in which case, they provide a backbone and context for formulating the user interface requirements.

The formal specification is then converted into a working prototype and is evaluated by the user. After a few iterations, which may result in changes and/or extensions to the specification, the specification is refined. Each refinement produces a prototype for evaluation and more iteration.

At some stage, the functional part of the system and the dialogue part are integrated. Integration can also take place before the refinement of the specification. The issue of when to integrate is really application dependent and is influenced by the way the project progresses. However, before integration starts, the user must be fully satisfied with the exhibited behaviour of the system.

The result of integration is a further prototype. Evaluation of this prototype will reveal whether a loop back to a previous stage is necessary or not. Once the system is integrated, it is repeatedly refined. Each refinement produces a complete delivery in the form of a prototype.

During the refinement process, abstract constructs in the system are replaced by more concrete ones. This process continues until the system is in its most concrete form and the last prototype may be tuned and released as the final system.

The development process can also be complemented with formal verification. This is not shown in Figure 4.1. Verification can be applied to the specification and refinement steps. Experience with the methodology, however, suggests that verification is usually cost-effective only when it is applied to the top level specification, after it has been evaluated and agreed upon. The reason for this is that top level specifications are very abstract and, therefore, easy to verify; but the more the system is refined the harder verification becomes. Also, errors in the top level specification are much more costly to correct than those in the refinements.

4.3 The EPROL wide spectrum language

EPROS is based on a wide spectrum language called EPROL which supports the formal specification, design and implementation of software system. EPROL is both a prototyping and a development language. It provides facilities for dealing with functional and dialogue aspects of a system, and is fully executable. Various facilities of EPROL are briefly described below. The syntax of EPROL is formally specified in Appendix A.

4.3.1   Functional specification notation

The functional specification notation of EPROL is based on META-IV – the formal specification notation of VDM [Bjorner and Jones 1978]. Specifications are written using mathematical notations and objects such as predicate calculus, sets, lists, mappings, abstract syntax, applicative combinators and pure functions. Side effects are specified by pre- and post-conditions over a class of states, in an abstraction called an operation. The main notation for specifying functionality is the abstract data type notation; it is used in specifying new data types [Rowe and Shoens 1983].

EPROL provides a number of extensions to the META-IV notation. Amongst these are: polymorphic types, operator mapping and operator distribution.

4.3.2   Dialogue specification notation

Dialogues in EPROL are specified by state transition diagrams. The notation for STDs is based on the graphical notation of Denert [Denert 1977], which distinguishes between three kinds of dialogue states. These are simple states, complex states and interaction points. A simple state refers to a computer action involving no interaction with the user. A complex state is an abstraction of an entire STD and may involve interaction with the user. An interaction point is where actual interaction with the user takes place. The notation of complex states allows dialogue specifications to be modularized in much the same way as functional specifications.

4.3.3   Design notation

The term *design* in EPROL refers to the refinement and modularization of a software system. In addition to abstract data types, four other kinds of modules are available for this purpose:

- **Functions** which roughly correspond to functions and procedures in modern programming languages. These are by nature imperative and can have a hierarchical structure.

- **Dialogues** which correspond to complex states in a dialogue specification. These are again imperative and can have a hierarchical structure.

- **Forms** which are used for defining electronic forms as abstract data types. These are non-hierarchical and object-oriented.

- **Clusters** which provide a powerful mechanism for extending the base language, introducing new abstractions and designing reusable software modules. Clusters have syntax driven interfaces and can also have a hierarchical structure.

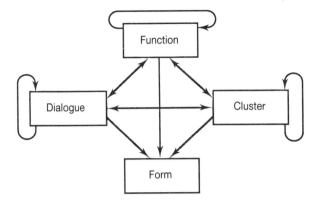

Figure 4.2 Module containment in EPROL.

The rules for the use of the above modules in hierarchical design are illustrated by Figure 4.2. Directed arrows should be read as 'may contain'.

4.3.4 Implementation notation

The implementation notation is based on a hybrid of C and Pascal, and is strongly typed and structured. Notably, all the constructs of META-IV are also supported by the implementation notation. So, the notation can be purely applicative, purely imperative, or a mixture of the two.

4.4 The architecture of the system

The architecture of EPROS is shown in Figure 4.3. The system is partitioned into 11 independent components. Central to the system is the EPROL compiler which implements the EPROL language. The compiler is itself divided into three major partitions which, in turn, cover the functional specification, the implementation, and the dialogue notations. These components are further modularized in a way that reflects the modularization of the notation. This open architecture has the advantage that the notation can be upgraded during the lifetime of the system with a minimum amount of effort

The second major part of the system is the interpreter, which sits directly on top of the compiler. The interpreter allows direct, interactive access to EPROL. The style of interaction is very much like a LISP environment, with the following exceptions.

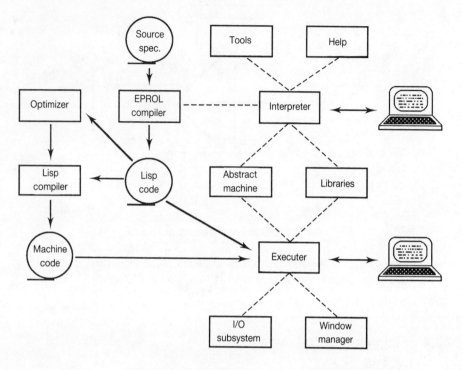

Figure 4.3 The architecture of EPROS.

- Two interaction modes are provided. The first, the expression mode, restricts the user to the functional specification notation. Computations causing side-effects are strictly prohibited in this mode. Also, the result of any interactively typed expression is immediately displayed (as in LISP). The second interaction mode, the statement mode, allows any form of computation. The display of end results in this mode is intentionally avoided; these may be optionally displayed using explicit I/O statements.

- The interpreter provides an interface to the symbol table of EPROL. This means that the user can find out what is currently defined. The interface also allows the user to remove unwanted definitions. Objects can be referred to either individually (by specifying an object's name), or collectively (by specifying a category, e.g., FUNCTIONs, CLUSTERs, etc.). The notation used for displaying objects is that of EPROL, and is handled by a dedicated pretty printer.

Using the interpreter, the user can interact with an already compiled EPROL file, or alternatively, create his own definitions.

The interpreter has direct interface to four other components of the system: the help subsystem, the tools, the abstract machine, and the libraries. The help subsystem provides interactive on-line help on a variety of topics, which include system commands, interpreter commands, and all syntactic components of EPROL (e.g., operators).

The tools part consists of a set of pre-developed tools. These currently include a cross-reference tool for EPROL, a highlighter for the neat display of EPROL files on the screen, and a pretty printer for pretty printing META-IV objects. In addition, new tools can be included with considerable ease, without disturbing the overall system.

The abstract machine part consists of a set of compact and highly optimized routines which implement the abstract objects of META-IV (i.e., sets, lists, mappings and trees). The libraries part consists of a set of predefined standard libraries for EPROL. (See Appendix A for a brief description of each library.) Both the abstract machine and the libraries are also shared by the executer component. The executer has the role of executing finished products (i.e. ones which have gone through design iteration). This component can be run independently of the rest to achieve greater efficiency by avoiding the overhead of unnecessary components.

The executer is, in turn, interfaced to the I/O subsystem and the window manager, which collectively support the dialogue mechanisms of EPROL. Both these are based on an internal notation which is hidden away from the user. This has the obvious advantage that these components can be changed (possibly in the event of porting the system to a new hardware configuration) without actually affecting the EPROL notation.

The remaining two components of the system (the optimizer and the LISP compiler) deal with the code generated by the EPROL compiler. The optimizer performs some straightforward improvements on the intermediate LISP code. The LISP compiler is a customized version of the standard Franz LISP compiler in the UNIX environment (i.e., Liszt). It simply translates the intermediate LISP code into machine code.

EPROS is implemented as two monolithic programs. The first program (eps) is the entire environment and includes all the components shown in Figure 4.3. The second program (epx) consists of the executor, the I/O subsystem, and the window manager. It is intended to be used for running complete systems only. The overall system has the following features.

- Compilation speed of approximately 1000 lines of EPROL source per minute.
- Full error detection, reporting and recovery.
- Separate compilation.
- Compiler switches.
- Compiler directives.
- Optional object code optimization.

- Various useful libraries.
- An extensive interactive synopsis and help facility.
- Various useful tools.
- An interface to the UNIX operating system, allowing interactive execution of UNIX commands from within the environment.

EPROS was developed and runs on a VAX-11/750 computer under Berkeley UNIX 4.2. It consists of 412 modules and occupies just under 20 000 lines of code. Two thirds of the system was written in LISP; the remaining third, which contains the main bottlenecks of the system, was written in C for the sake of efficiency.

4.5 Summary

This chapter has presented an overview of the EPROS system, which will be described in more detail in later chapters. The system is based on a wide spectrum language, EPROL, which contains facilities for expressing dialogue specification, functional specification and implementation. The architecture of the system has been designed so that all the prototyping approaches described in Chapter 2 can be used.

Chapter 5
Functional Specification

The specification of a software system is divided into two parts. The first part specifies the functional requirements of the system and is described in this chapter. The second part specifies the user interface requirements of the system and is described in Chapter 8. The notations and methods presented also cover the design stage where decisions about how the requirements are to be realized are made. As stated earlier, the functional specification notation of EPROL is largely based on VDM, a brief outline of which is given below.

5.1 The Vienna development method

VDM is a constructive or abstract model-oriented formal specification and design method based on discrete mathematics [Jones 1980a, Bjorner and Jones 1982,

45

Jones 1986]. The formal specification language of VDM is known as META-IV and is extensively described in [Bjorner and Jones 1978]. VDM only considers the functional specification and development of software systems. Other aspects, such as the user interface, have to be developed using other notations and methodologies.

Very briefly, in VDM, a system is developed according to the following steps.

> specify the system formally.
> prove that the specification is consistent.
> **do**
> > refine and decompose the specification (realization).
> > prove that the realization satisfies the previous specification.
> **until** the realization is as concrete as a program.
> revise the above steps.

In VDM, a specification is written as a constructive specification of a data type, by defining a class of objects and a set of operations to act upon these objects while preserving their essential properties; such a data type is known as an abstract data type. A program is itself specified as an abstract data type by considering it to consist of a set of operations on a class of states which model the program variables. The notion of state is, therefore, made explicit in VDM; this is in contrast to other specification methods such as those of the algebraic approach.

A number of data types and constructs are considered as primitives in VDM. These are familiar mathematical objects such as sets, lists, mappings, abstract syntax and functions. In addition, the notation of first order logic is used extensively. The following sections describe these notations briefly. Section 5.6 describes the way abstract data types are specified, developed and verified.

5.2 Logic

The notation of logic is based on a simple set containing two elements only, i.e., TRUE and FALSE. The set is called Bool, so:

$Bool = \{TRUE, FALSE\}$

TRUE and FALSE are often called **truth values**. Every expression in logic (also called a Boolean expression or a predicate) has a truth value. Logic provides a number of operators, usually referred to as **Boolean operators**, for writing predicates. These are: not, and, or, implication and equivalence operators, represented by the symbols ¬, ∧, ∨, ⇒ and ⇔, respectively. The Boolean operators have the following meanings.

¬x   is true if x is false, and false otherwise.
x ∧ y   is true if both x and y are true, and false otherwise.
x ∨ y   is false if both x and y are false, and true otherwise.
x ⇒ y   is false if x is true and y is false, and true otherwise.
x ⇔ y   is true if both x and y are either true or false, and false otherwise.

It follows, therefore, that:

x ⇒ y ≡ ¬x ∨ y
x ⇔ y ≡ (x ∧ y) ∨ (¬x ∧ ¬y)

5.2.1   Quantifiers

Occasionally in logic, we would like to state that a certain predicate holds for various values of some variable. This is where quantifiers may be useful. There are two quantifiers in logic called the **universal** and the **existential** quantifiers, represented here by the symbols ∀ and ∃, respectively. Predicates written using quantifiers are called **quantified expressions**, examples are

(∀ x ∈ s: p(x))
(∃ x ∈ s: p(x))

where s is a set and p is a predicate over x. The former expression states that for any x in s, p(x) is true. The latter expression states that there is a x in s such that p(x) is true. It follows, therefore, that:

¬(∀ x ∈ s: p(x)) ⇔ (∃ x ∈ s: ¬p(x))
¬(∃ x ∈ s: p(x)) ⇔ (∀ x ∈ s: ¬p(x))

A special case of the existential quantifier is the **unique existential** quantifier represented by ∃!; for example,

(∃! x ∈ s: p(x))

states that there is a unique x in s such that p(x) holds.

In the above examples, x is called a **bound variable**, s is called a **constraint**, and p is called the **body** of the quantified expression. In general, a quantified expression may have more than one bound variable. Such expressions

can always be written as a sequence of nested quantified expressions with single
bound variables; for example:

$$(\forall \; x1,x2,\dots,xn \in S: p)$$
$$\Leftrightarrow (\forall \; x1 \in S: (\forall \; x2 \in S: \dots (\forall \; xn \in S: p)\dots))$$

5.3 Abstract objects

This section briefly describes certain abstract object classes which are extensively
used in specifications. Each object class will be described briefly, and informally,
together with its associated set of operators.

5.3.1 Sets

A set is an unordered collection of objects with no repetitions. An object in a set is
said to be a **member** of that set. A set may be defined *explicitly* by enumerating all
its members. For example,

```
{Japan, Italy, Canada, Germany}
```

specifies a set of countries. Sets which consist of a range of integers may be
abbreviated to a range; for example:

```
{10,11,12,13,14} = {10:14}
```

A set may also be defined *implicitly*, by defining a general member of the set. For
example,

```
{sqrt(x): x ∈ s ∧ is_even(x)}
```

specifies the set of square roots of even integers in s. In general, an implicit set is
written as

```
{e(x1,...,xn): p(x1,...,xn)}
```

where e is an expression called the **generator** and p is a predicate called the
constraint, both over variables $x1,\dots,xn$ which are called the **bound
variables**.

Here is a summary of the set operators and their meanings:

$e \in s$	is true if e is a member of s, and false otherwise.
$s1 \subseteq s2$	is true if $s1$ is a subset of $s2$, and false otherwise.
	Formally, $s1 \subseteq s2 \Leftrightarrow (\forall\ e \in s1: e \in s2)$.
$s1 \subset s2$	is true if $s1$ is a proper subset of $s2$, and false otherwise.
	Formally, $s1 \subset s2 \Leftrightarrow s1 \subseteq s2 \wedge s1 \ne s2$.
$s1 \cup s2$	denotes the union of $s1$ and $s2$ (i.e., the set of objects which are either in $s1$, or in $s2$, or both).
	Formally, $s1 \cup s2 = \{e: e \in s1 \vee e \in s2\}$.
$s1 \cap s2$	denotes the intersection of $s1$ and $s2$ (i.e., the set of objects which are in both $s1$ and $s2$).
	Formally, $s1 \cap s2 = \{e: e \in s1 \wedge e \in s2\}$.
$s1 - s2$	denotes the difference of $s1$ and $s2$ (i.e., the set of objects which are in $s1$ but not in $s2$).
	Formally, $s1 - s2 = \{e: e \in s \wedge e \notin s2\}$.
card s	denotes the cardinality of s (i.e., the number of members of s).
power s	denotes the power set of s (i.e., the set of all subsets of s).
	Formally, *power* $s = \{e: e \subseteq s\}$.
$\cup$ ss	denotes the distributed union of ss (i.e., the union of all sets in a set of sets ss).
	Formally, $\cup\ ss = \{e: (\exists\ s \in ss: e \in s)\}$.

Two additional operators are selection and unique selection, represented by ι and $\iota!$, respectively. These have a similar syntax to quantifiers; for example,

$$(\iota\ x \in s: p(x))$$

produces an element of s (if any) for which p holds, in a pseudo non-deterministic manner. Similarly,

$$(\iota!\ x \in s: q(x))$$

produces the unique element of s (if any) for which q holds.

5.3.2   Lists

A list is an ordered collection of objects which may contain repetitions. An object in a list is said to be an **element** of that list. Like sets, a list may be defined explicitly by enumerating all its elements. For example,

<Austin, Fiat, Rover, Fiat, Ford>

specifies a list of cars. Alternatively, a list may be defined implicitly. For example,

<i: i ∈ s ∧ (∀ j ∈ {2:i}: i%j ≠ 0)>

produces the list of all those integers in s which are prime (% is the remainder operator). In general, an implicit list definition is written as

<e(x1,...,xn): p(x1,...,xn)>

and is similar to an implicit set definition.

Here is a summary of the list operators and their meanings:

l[i]	denotes the ith element of list l (starting at 1).
l1 ⌢ l2	denotes the concatenation of l1 and l2 (i.e., the list consisting of elements of l1 followed by elements of l2, in the same order as l1 and l2 and having a length equal to the length of l1 plus the length of l2).
hd l	denotes the head of l (i.e., the first element of l). Formally, hd l = l[1].
tl l	denotes the tail of l (i.e., the list consisting of all elements of l except the first, in the same order as l). Formally, tl l ⌢ tl l = l.
len l	denotes the length of l (i.e., the number of elements of l including the repetitions, if any).
elems l	denotes the elements of l (i.e., the set consisting of elements of l).
inds l	denotes the set of indices of l. Formally, inds l = {1:len l}.
conc ll	denotes the distributed concatenation of the lists in the list of lists ll. Formally, ll = <l1,l2,...,ln> ⇔ conc ll = l1 ⌢ l2 ⌢...⌢ ln.

Two additional list operators are map and dist. These have an unusual syntax and are used for mapping or distributing an operator (or a function) over a list, where the operator (or the function) must be unary or binary for map, and binary for dist. Here are two examples of their use:

map(card: <{},{1,2},{5}>) = <0,2,1>
dist(+: <5,10,20>) = 35

Combination of map and dist provides a succinct notation for specification. For example, a predicate denoting that the elements of a list of numbers are sorted in ascending order may be written as

$dist(\wedge, <: 1)$

which is equivalent to

$dist(\wedge: map(<: 1))$

Nested map and dist applications may be abbreviated according to the conventions.

$map(f1, f2, \ldots, fn: 1) = map(f1: map(f2: \ldots map(fn: 1)\ldots))$
$dist(f, g1, \ldots, gn: 1) = dist(f: map(g1: \ldots map(gn: 1)\ldots))$

where fs and gs may be operators or functions.

5.3.3 Mappings

A mapping (or map) is a finite function. It maps the elements of a set, called its **domain**, to the elements of a set, called its **range**. A mapping can be defined explicitly by enumerating how individual elements of its domain are mapped to individual elements of its range. For example,

[John ↦ 20, Peter ↦ 12, Steve ↦ 25]

maps three persons to their ages. As with sets and lists, a mapping can also be defined implicitly. For example,

[i ↦ i*i: i ∈ s]

maps every number in s to its square. In general, an implicit mapping is written as:

[e1(x1,...xn) ↦ e2(x1,...,xn): p(x1,...,xn)]

Here is a summary of the mapping operators and their meanings:

m(x)   denotes an element of the range of m to which x is mapped by m.
m1 + m2   denotes the mapping which is the result of merging m1 and m2
             provided the domains of m1 and m2 are disjoint.

Formally, $m1 + m2 = [e \mapsto f: e \in dom\ m1 \wedge f = m1(e) \vee$
$$e \in dom\ m2 \wedge f = m2(e)].$$

m1 † m2   denotes the mapping which is the result of overwriting m1 by m2.
Formally, $m1\ †\ m2 = [e \mapsto f: e \in (dom\ m1 - dom\ m2) \wedge f =$
$$m1(e) \vee e \in dom\ m2 \wedge f = m2(e)].$$

m1 ∘ m2   denotes the composition of m1 and m2 provided the range of m2 is a subset of the domain of m1.
Formally, $m1\ ∘\ m2 = [e \mapsto f: e \in dom\ m2 \wedge$
$$f = m1(m2(e))].$$

m ◁ s   denotes the mapping which is identical to m but whose domain is restricted to the set s.
Formally, $m\ ◁\ s = [e \mapsto m(x): x \in (dom\ m \cap s)].$

m ◁ s   denotes the mapping which is identical to m but from whose domain the elements of the set s have been removed.
Formally, $m\ ◁\ s = [e \mapsto m(x): x \in (dom\ m - s)].$

dom m   denotes the domain of m.

rng m   denotes the range of m.

merge ms   denotes the distributed merge of the mappings in the set of mappings ms, provided the domains of the mappings are disjoint.
Formally, $merge\ ms = [e \mapsto (\imath!\ m \in ms: e \in dom\ m)(e)$
$$: e \in \cup\{dom\ m: m \in ms\}].$$

5.4 Abstract syntax

Certain elementary domains are predefined in EPROL, these are:

Nat	Natural numbers.
Nat0	Natural numbers including zero.
Int	Integer numbers.
Real	Real numbers.
Bool	Booleans, i.e., {TRUE, FALSE}.
Char	Characters.
Str	Strings.

The notation of abstract syntax allows one to define other, possibly more complex domains. An abstract syntax definition consists of one or more abstract syntax rules. A rule has the general form

```
domain_id = domain_expr
```

which introduces a new domain called `domain_id`, denoted by `domain_expr`. A domain expression is an expression consisting of domain names and domain operators. The operators of the abstract syntax notation are as follows.

D-*set*   denotes a class of objects where each object is a subset of D.
                Formally, $s \in$ D-*set* $\Leftrightarrow$ $s \subseteq$ D.
D-*list*   denotes a class of objects, each object is a list of some objects in D.
                Formally, $l \in$ D-list $\Leftrightarrow$ *elems* $l \subseteq$ D.
D1 → D2   denotes a class of objects where each object is a mapping whose
                domain is a subset of D1 and whose range is a subset of D2.
                Formally, $m \in$ (D1 → D2) $\Leftrightarrow$ *dom* $m \subseteq$ D1 $\wedge$ *rng* $m \subseteq$ D2.
D1 | D2   denotes a class of objects where each object is either in D1, or in D2,
                or both. Formally, $d \in$ (D1 | D2) $\Leftrightarrow$ $d \in$ D $\vee$ $d \in$ D2.
[D]   denotes a class of objects where each object is either in D or is just
                the NIL object. Formally, $d \in$ [D] $\Leftrightarrow$ $d \in$ D $\vee$ d = NIL.

Round brackets may also be used in domain expressions for grouping and to enhance readability. Two domain definition examples are given below.

```
D1 = Int-set → Bool-list-set
D2 = (D1 → Str) → (D1 | Int | Real)
```

Each object in D1 is a mapping from the power set of integers to the sets of lists of Booleans. Each object in D2 is a mapping from the mappings which map D1 to strings, to either an object in D1, or an integer, or a real.

Abstract syntax rules may also be recursive (i.e., refer to themselves). For example,

```
D = Int → [D]
```

defines a domain called D, where each object in D is a mapping from integers to either D itself, or to NIL.

5.4.1 Trees

The notation so far described does not allow us to define structured objects. A structured object is an object which consists of a number of components. The domain of such objects is called a **tree**. These are specified by replacing the =

symbol, in an abstract syntax definition, by the symbol ::. For example,

```
D :: Int, Str-list, Real-set
```

defines a tree domain called D where each object in D has exactly three components. These being, in order, an integer, a string list, and a real set. An object in a tree domain is usually called a tree **branch**. A special function called mk may be used to make such objects, e.g.:

```
mk-D(1,<"ab","ef">,{1.5}) ∈ D
```

Individual components of a tree domain may be named as shown below.

```
D :: i: Int, sl: Str-list, rs: Real-set
```

Given this domain definition, individual components of an object in D may be specified by adding the component name to the end of the object. For example, let

```
d = mk-D(2,<"hi","there">,{1.5})
```

then

```
d.i = 2
d.sl = <"hi","there">
```

It is also possible to name only selected components:

```
D :: Int, sl: Str-list, Real-set
```

A tree may also be defined using the following notation

```
D = tree(Int, Str-list, Real-set)
```

which is equivalent to

```
D :: Int, Str-list, Real-set
```

The former form is useful for defining nested trees, sets of trees, etc. For instance,

```
P = tree(n: Str, a: Int, p: tree(str-set, Int))
```

is a shorter way of saying

```
P :: n: Str, a: Int, p: Q
Q :: Str-set, Int
```

and avoiding the definition of the new domain Q.

5.5 Combinators

EPROL provides a number of combinators for use in specifications. These do not cause any side-effects; they simply return a value. Each combinator is informally and briefly described below.

5.5.1 The let expression

The let expression is used for naming one or more expressions within another expression. The simplest form of a let expression is

```
let id = expr1 in
    expr2
```

which means that every occurrence of id in expr2 will be bound to the value of expr1. More generally,

```
let id1 = expr1,
    id2 = expr2,

    idn = exprn in
    expr
```

binds id1, id2, ..., idn to expr1, expr2, ..., exprn, respectively and in parallel, in expr.

The let combinator may also be used for naming individual components of a tree. Consider the following abstract syntax definition.

```
Student :: name: Str, age: Nat, id: Nat0;
```

Now suppose st ∈ Student and that st = ("Phil", 25, 10516), then

```
let (n,a,id) = st in
    n = "Phil" ∧ a = 25 ∧ id = 10516
```

is true. In this example n is bound to the first field in the tree (i.e., "Phil"), a to the second field (i.e., 25), and id to the last field (i.e., 10516).

5.5.2 The if-then-else expression

The simplest form of a conditional expression is the if-then-else expression. The general form for this combinator is:

> if bool_expr *then* expr1 *else* expr2

The overall value of this expression is the value of expr1 if bool_expr evaluates to TRUE, and the value of expr2 if it evaluates to FALSE.

5.5.3 The mac expression

This is McCarthy's expression and has the general form:

```
mac {
      bool_expr1 → expr1,
      bool_expr2 → expr2,
      :
      bool_exprn → exprn,
}
```

It specifies a multi-branch conditional expression. The bool_expr expressions on the left hand side are evaluated in the order they appear. If bool_expri evaluates to TRUE then expri will be evaluated and its value will be returned as the value of the overall mac expression. At least one bool_expri must evaluate to TRUE.

5.5.4 The cases expression

This is similar to the mac expression and has the general form:

```
cases exprs {
      lexpr1 → rexpr1,
      lexpr2 → rexpr2
      :
      lexprn → rexprn,
}
```

First exprs is evaluated. Then the lexpr expressions are evaluated in the order they occur. If lexpri = exprs then rexpri will be evaluated and its value will be returned as the value of the cases expression. At least one lexpri must have the same value as exprs. As a convention, the last lexpr may be simply TRUE to ensure this.

5.6 Abstract data types

To be concise when specifying software systems, one must depart from the elementary data types of a specification language and instead 'create' data types which match the problem at hand more closely and more naturally. Such a data type is called an **abstract data type** and is characterized by its private set of operations.

5.6.1 Specification

An abstract data type is specified by a class of states and a set of private operations to act upon the states. It introduces a new data type, where an object of this type can be manipulated only through the specified operations. The class of states is denoted by a domain, usually restricted by a predicate called the data type invariant which must be preserved by the operations.

In EPROL, abstract data types are specified by ADT modules. The general structure of an ADT module is shown in Figure 5.1.

```
ADT  adt_id
   DOM   ... private domain definitions ...
   TYPE ... private type clause definitions ...
   AUX   ... private auxiliary function definitions ...
   OPS
      :
      private operation definitions
      :
END  adt_id
```

Figure 5.1 The general structure of an ADT module.

The first three parts in the definition (i.e., DOM, TYPE and AUX) are optional. The DOM part introduces new domains; for example,

```
DOM    Product = Pname → Pid;
       Pname = Str;
       Pid = Int;
```

defines three new domains called Product, Pname and Pid. The object class (i.e., class of states) for the abstract data type itself must be defined here.

The AUX part is used for defining new auxiliary functions. Every function defined here must have its type clause already defined in the TYPE part. For example,

```
TYPE    is_disjoint: Int-set, Int-set → Bool;
        is_empty: Int-set → Bool;
AUX     is_disjoint(s1,s2) ≙ s1 ∩ s2 = {};
        is_empty(s) ≙ s = {};
```

defines two auxiliary functions called is_disjoint and is_empty. The domain of a function can be restricted by a pre-condition; this is a predicate over the domain of the function which must hold before the function is applied. For example, a function called max which takes a set of integers and returns the largest integer in the set may be defined as

```
TYPE    max: Int-set → Int;
AUX     pre-max(s) ≙ s ≠ {};
        max(s) ≙ (ι e ∈ s: (∀ e1 ∈ s: e ⩾ e1));
```

where the pre-condition indicates that max is not defined for the empty set.

If an abstract data type has a data type invariant then it must be defined in the AUX part. For example,

```
AUX inv-Product(p) ≙ dom p ≠ {};
```

defines a data type invariant for an abstract data type called Product.

The last part in an ADT module is OPS and specifies one or more operations for the abstract data type. The general structure of an operation specification is shown in Figure 5.2. Each operation acts upon the class of states of the abstract data type. In addition, an operation may take arguments and/or return a result, as in a function. This is specified by the type clause of the operation. For example,

```
OP: Dom1, Dom2 → Dom3
```

```
OP_ID: ... operation type clause ...;
  pre (...) ≙ ... pre-condition predicate ...;
  post (...) ≙ ... post-condition predicate ...;

     :
     private auxiliary function definitions
     :
END OP_ID
```

Figure 5.2 The general structure of an operation specification.

specifies that operation OP takes two arguments in Dom1 and Dom2 and returns a result in Dom3. An operation is specified in terms of two predicates called the pre- and the post-condition. The pre-condition is optional and is assumed to be TRUE if it is not present. It is a predicate over the states and any arguments the operation may take, and specifies a condition which must hold before the operation is applied. Alternatively, it may be specified as a list of exception clauses, where each exception clause maps a predicate to an exception name. The overall pre-condition will then be a conjunction of the negation of individual exception predicates (see Appendix B for examples).

The post-condition specifies a condition which must hold after the operation is applied. It is a predicate over the states before and after the operation is applied, as well as any arguments and result the operation may take and produce. Consider a general operation OP over the states St with the following type clause.

```
OP: Dom1, Dom2, ..., Domn → Res;
```

The pre- and post-conditions will have the following implicit type clauses.

```
pre:  St, Dom1, Dom2, ..., Domn → Bool;
post: St, Dom1, Dom2, ..., Domn, St, Res → Bool;
```

The position of a parameter in a condition indicates its actual domain. So, for example,

```
pre(st,arg1,arg2,...,argn) ≙ ... ;
post(st,arg1,arg2,...,argn,st',res) ≙ ... ;
```

indicates that
```
st, st' ∈ St
arg1 ∈ Dom1, arg2 ∈ Dom2, ..., argn ∈ Domn
```

```
res ∈ Res
```

where st and st' refer to the 'states before' and 'states after'.

In EPROL, a parameter can be replaced by a minus symbol according to the following conventions:

- When replacing the 'states before' parameter it implies that we are not interested in the value of the states before the operation is applied.

- When replacing the 'states after' parameter it implies that the value of the states will not be changed by the operation.

- When replacing any other parameter it implies that the value of that parameter is not relevant to the specified condition.

An operation can also have its own private auxiliary functions. Such functions may appear inside an operation specification, just after the post-condition.

5.6.2   Refinement

The initial specification of an abstract data type is written as abstractly as possible while ensuring that it captures all the required properties of the problem at hand. The abstract data type is then developed by the process of **data refinement**, whereby it is realized in a more concrete form. This process produces a so-called **representation** of the abstract data type. The process consists of four steps, each supported by mathematical proof:

- Find a more concrete class of states for the abstract data type.
- Redefine the data type invariant for the new class of states.
- Find a function which maps each object in the new class of states to its corresponding object in the previous class of states. This is called a **retrieve** function and relates a representation to its abstraction.
- Redefine each operation of the abstract data type for the new class of states.

Refinement is an iterative process which results in successively more concrete representations of an abstract data type. It is repeated until the final representation is in a sufficiently concrete form.

The original specification and each subsequent refinement can be shown to be internally correct. In addition, one can show that a representation is correct with respect to its abstraction.

5.6.3   Verification rules

VDM provides a number of useful rules for verifying the correctness of abstract data type specifications and their refinements. These are directly used in EPROL and are briefly described below. For a more detailed discussion of the rules see [Jones 1980] or [Jones 1986].

Let D be an abstract data type, having a class of states S, a data type invariant inv and a set of operations P1,P2,...,Pn. Operation Pi is **valid** if it preserves the data type invariant, i.e., for any s in S:

Rule 1
$pre\text{-}Pi(s,args) \wedge inv(s) \wedge post\text{-}Pi(s,args,s',res) \Leftrightarrow inv(s')$

Let D1 be a refinement of D, having a class of states S1, a data type invariant inv1 and a set of operations Q1,Q2,...,Qn corresponding to P1,P2,...,Pn, respectively. Also, let retr be the retrieve function from S1 to S:

$retr\colon S1 \rightarrow S$

The retrieve function is **total** over valid states (i.e., states which satisfy the data type invariant inv1) if

Rule 2
$(\forall\ s1 \in S1\colon inv1(s1) \Rightarrow (\exists\ s \in S\colon s{=}retr(s1)) \wedge inv(retr(s1)))$

and S1 is an **adequate** representation of S if

Rule 3
$(\forall\ s \in S\colon inv(s) \Rightarrow (\exists\ s1 \in S1\colon inv1(s1) \wedge s = retr(s1)))$

Operation Qi **models** operation Pi if:

Rule 4
$(\forall\ s1 \in S1\colon inv1(s1) \wedge pre\text{-}Pi(retr(s1),args)$
$\Rightarrow pre\text{-}Qi(s1,args))$

and

Rule 5

($\forall$ s1 $\in$ S1: *invI*(s1) $\land$ *pre*–Qi(s1,args) $\land$*post*(s1,args,s1',res)
$\Rightarrow$ *post*–Pi(*retr*(s1),args,*retr*(s1'),res))

Proof of correctness reduces to showing that Rule 1 holds for each specification and that Rules 2 – 5 hold for each specification with respect to its abstraction.

5.6.4 Polymorphic types

All abstractions so far described such as functions, operations and abstract data types required a precise domain specification. This in turn limits their utility. Consider, for example, a function called largest which returns the largest set in a set of sets and has the following definition.

```
largest: Int-set-set → Int-set;
pre-largest(ss) ≙ ss ≠ {};
largest(ss) ≙ (℩ s ∈ ss: (∀ s1 ∈ ss: card s ⩾ card s1));
```

This function is only valid for sets of integer sets.

More desirable, and certainly more useful, would be a function which would work for sets of sets of any type. Such functions may be defined using polymorphic types [Turner 1985]. The function largest, for example, may be defined polymorphically by defining its type clause to be:

```
largest: *-set-set → *-set;
```

More complicated functions may require more than one polymorphic type. Additional types may be specified by **, *** and so on. To give an example, suppose we want to define the map remove operator ◁ as a function. It may be defined as the following polymorphic function.

```
m_remove: * → **, *-set → * → **;
m_remove(m,s) ≙ [x ↦ m(x) : x ∈ (dom m - s)]
```

Here ** specifies a type which may be different from the one specified by *, as shown by the following applications of m_remove.

```
m_remove([1 ↦ "small", 10 ↦ "big", 100 ↦ "very big"], {10})
= [1 ↦ "small",100 ↦ "very big"]
m_remove([1 ↦ {1}, 2 ↦ {1,2}, 3 ↦ {1,2,3}], {1,2,5})
= [3 ↦ {1,2,3}]
```

In the first example * becomes Int and ** becomes Str. In the second example *
becomes Int and ** becomes Int-set. Every application of m_remove involves
three type checkings, as illustrated by the diagram below.

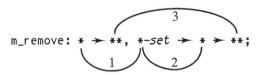

The use of polymorphic types is not restricted to functions. They may also be used
in operations, abstract data types and other forms of abstraction described in the rest
of this book. Polymorphic types are especially suitable for writing general purpose
abstractions, which crop up in a variety of specifications, without losing the
advantages of type checking.

5.7   Summary

This chapter has described how system functionality can be expressed
using mathematics. In particular, it has shown how a system's state can
be specified and how objects such as sets and lists can be used to model
stored data. The Vienna development method was also described. This
is a mathematical technique whereby an initial abstract description of a
software system is decomposed into specifications which lie nearer the
storage facilities of the computer. The chapter terminated with a
discussion of the proof rules that need to be satisfied when using the
Vienna development method.

Chapter 6
Case Study 1
A Cross Usage Program

6.1 Problem specification
6.2 Refinement of specification

6.3 Discussion
6.4 Summary

This chapter illustrates, by means of a realistic example, how a formal specification may be developed, refined, evaluated and formally verified in EPROS. The interactive evaluation of a formal specification can serve two purposes. Firstly, it can provide a means of observing the behaviour of the specified system in order to see whether it is indeed the one desired. Secondly, it may serve as a cheap and fast way of detecting design errors. The example given here exhibits the potential of the approach for both applications.

6.1 Problem specification

The program to be specified is a software tool that records the relationships between the modules of a software system. An informal statement of the requirements is given below.

A program is required which records the **uses** and **used-by**

relationships between the modules of a software system. It should
allow the user to do the following.

- Add a module to the system.
- Delete a module from the system.
- List what modules a given module may use.
- List what modules may use a given module.
- List all recursive modules.

Let us call this program the 'Cross Usage' program. Our first task is to find a
suitable object class that can model the problem. Let us call the object class Xusage;
it can be modelled by a mapping which maps every module in a system to the set of
modules it may use, i.e.:

Xusage = Module → Module-*set*;

At this point, we shall not specify the domain Module. Every object in Module is
understood to correspond to a module in a system. Module, in other words, is the
set of all possible modules in software systems. As an example, consider the
following object in Xusage.

```
[mod1 ↦ {mod2,mod3},
 mod2 ↦ {},
 mod3 ↦ {}]
```

It represents a system which has the structure diagram shown in Figure 6.1, where
mod1 may call mod2 and mod3, and mod2 and mod3 may not call any other module.
Obviously, given that s is the set of modules a module m may call, then s
must be contained in the domain of the mapping, i.e.,

($\forall$ m $\in$ *dom* xu: xu(m) $\subseteq$ *dom* xu)

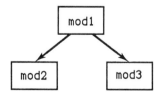

Figure 6.1 A simple structure diagram.

where xu is the mapping. This is specified by the following data type invariant.

$$inv\text{-}Xusage(xu) \triangleq U(rng\ xu) \subseteq dom\ xu$$

Now let us specify the operations of abstract data type Xusage. The first operation is very simple; it just initializes the mapping to an empty map:

```
INIT: → ;
    post(-,xu') ≜ xu' = [];
END INIT
```

The next operation to be specified, adds a module to the system. It takes a module and a set of modules that the module may use and adds them to the mapping:

```
ADD_MOD: Module, Module-set → ;
    pre(xu,mod,-) ≜ mod ∉ dom xu ∨ xu(mod) = {};
    post(xu,mod,uses,xu') ≜
        xu' = xu + [m ↦ {}: m ∈ (uses - dom xu)] † [mod ↦
                        uses];
END ADD_MOD
```

The pre-condition specifies either that the module (to be added) should not be already in the mapping or, if it is, it should not be using any other module at the moment. The post-condition specifies that the mapping after the operation is applied will be equal to the mapping before the operation is applied, merged with an implicit mapping which maps each new module in uses to the empty set, and then overwritten by an explicit mapping which maps the module to be added to uses.

The next operation deletes a module from the system:

```
DEL_MOD: Module → ;
    pre(xu,mod) ≜ mod ∈ dom xu;
    post(xu,mod,xu') ≜
        xu' = [m → xu(m) - {mod} : m ∈ (dom xu - {mod})];
END DEL_MOD
```

Obviously a module to be deleted must already be present in the system, hence the pre-condition. The post-condition specifies that the effect of the operation will be that all occurrences of the deleted module will be removed from the right hand side of the mapping and the particular entry for the module itself will be totally removed from the mapping.

The next two operations are trivial. The first is USES which returns the set of modules a given module may use:

```
USES: Module → Module-set;
    pre(xu,mod) ≙ mod ∈ dom xu;
    post(xu,mod,-,ms) ≙ ms = xu(mod);
END USES
```

The second operation, USED_BY, returns the set of modules that may use a given module:

```
USED_BY: Module → Module-set;
    pre(xu,mod) ≙ mod ∈ dom xu;
    post(xu,mod,-,ms) ≙
        ms = {m : m ∈ dom xu ∧ mod ∈ xu(m)};
END USED_BY
```

The last operation produces the set of recursive modules in a system:

```
REC_MOD: → Module-set;
    post(xu,-,ms) ≙
        ms = {m: m ∈ dom xu ∧ reaches(m,m,xu)};

    pre-reaches(m1,m2,xu) ≙ m1 ∈ dom xu ∧ m2 ∈ dom xu;
        reaches(m1,m2,xu) ≙ m2 ∈ xu(m1) ∨
                        (∃ m ∈ xu(m1): reaches(m,m2,xu));
END REC_MOD
```

The post-condition uses an auxiliary function called reaches which has the following type clause. It describes a function from Module, Module, Xusage to Bool.

```
reaches: Module, Module, Xusage → Bool;
```

This function is defined to be local to the operation and returns TRUE if a module can reach another module through a sequence of one or more calls. We observe the conciseness of the post-condition: the set of modules m in the system such that m can somehow reach itself.

Having specified our abstract data type the next stage in the development process involves the evaluation of the specification. Here, we examine the behaviour of the system by executing the specification. The following is a simple evaluation session based on setting up and manipulating the system shown in Figure 6.2. (See Appendix A for a description of the commands and the prompts.) The domain Module is assumed to be of type Str. EPROS response appears in bold.

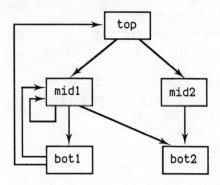

Figure 6.2 A more complicated structure diagram.

```
stat> VAR x: Xusage;;              /* define x of type Xusage */
stat> INIT(x);                     /* initialize x */
stat> `x;                          /* check the contents of x */
[ ]
stat> ADD_MOD(x,"top",{"mid1","mid2"});     /* add modules */
stat> ADD_MOD(x,"mid1",{"mid1","bot1","bot2"});
stat> ADD_MOD(x,"mid2",{"bot2"});
stat> ADD_MOD(x,"bot1",{"top","mid1"});
stat> `x;                          /* check the contents of x */
["bot2"  ↦  {},
 "mid2"  ↦  {"bot2"},
 "top"   ↦  {"mid2","mid1"},
 "mid1"  ↦  {"bot2","bot1","mid1"},
 "bot1"  ↦  {"mid1","top"}]
stat> USES(x,"top");               /* list modules that top uses */
{"mid1","mid2"}
stat> USED_BY(x,"mid1");           /* list modules that use mid1 */
{"top","mid1","bot1"}
stat> REC_MOD(x);                  /* list recursive modules */
{"top","mid1","bot1"}
stat> DEL_MOD(x,"mid2");           /* delete module mid2 */
stat> `x;                          /* check the contents of x */
["bot2"  ↦  {},
 "top"   ↦  {"mid1"},
 "mid1"  ↦  {"bot2","bot1","mid1"},
 "bot1"  ↦  {"mid1","top"}]
stat>
```

Having convinced ourselves that the exhibited behaviour is indeed the one desired, we now verify the specification. Since this is the first specification of the system, all that we can verify at this stage is that each operation preserves the data type invariant.

Lemma 6.1

Operation INIT is valid.

Proof

For this operation we observe that

$$post(xu,xu') \Rightarrow inv(xu') \qquad (1)$$

since

$$
\begin{aligned}
inv(xu') \quad &= inv([]) \\
&= \cup(rng \; []) \subseteq dom \; [] \\
&= \{\} \subseteq \{\} = \text{TRUE}
\end{aligned}
$$

From **(1)** it follows that

$$pre(xu) \wedge inv(xu) \wedge post(xu,xu') \Rightarrow inv(xu')$$

which proves that INIT is valid. $\qquad\square$

Lemma 6.2

Operation ADD_MOD is valid.

Proof

We must show that:

$$
pre(xu,mod,uses) \wedge inv(xu) \wedge post(xu,mod,uses,xu') \Rightarrow \\
inv(xu')
$$

Now

$$inv(xu') = inv(xu + m1 \dagger m2)$$

where

$$
\begin{aligned}
m1 &= [m \mapsto \{\}: m \in (uses - dom \; xu)] \\
m2 &= [mod \mapsto uses]
\end{aligned}
$$

Hence

$$
\begin{aligned}
inv(xu') &= inv(xu + m1 \dagger m2) \\
&= \cup rng(xu + m1 \dagger m2) \subseteq dom \; (xu + m1 \dagger m2)
\end{aligned}
$$

From *pre* it follows that

$$\cup rng(xu + m1 \dagger m2) = \cup(rng \; xu) \cup \cup(rng \; m1 \dagger m2)$$

Hence

```
inv(xu')
= (∪(rng xu) ∪ ∪rng(m1 † m2)) ⊆ dom (xu + m1 † m2)
= (∪(rng xu) ∪ uses) ⊆ (dom xu ∪ dom m1 ∪ dom m2)
= (∪(rng xu) ∪ uses) ⊆ (dom xu ∪ (uses-dom xu) ∪ {mod})
= (∪(rng xu) ∪ uses) ⊆ (dom xu ∪ uses ∪ {mod})
```

which is true since using $inv(xu)$,

$$∪(rng\ xu) ⊆ dom\ xu$$

and completes the proof.

Lemma 6.3

Operation DEL_MOD is valid.

Proof

Consider the stronger condition

$$inv(xu) ∧ post(xu,mod,xu') ⇒ inv(xu')$$

where

$$inv(xu') ≜ ∪(rng\ xu') ⊆ dom\ xu'$$

Now (using *post*)

$$∪(rng\ xu') ⊆ ∪(rng\ xu) - \{mod\} \tag{1}$$

and (using *inv*)

$$∪(rng\ xu) - \{mod\} ⊆ dom\ xu - \{mod\} \tag{2}$$

also (using *post*)

$$dom\ xu - \{mod\} = dom\ xu' \tag{3}$$

From **(1)**,**(2)** and **(3)** it follows that

$$∪(rng\ xu') ⊆ dom\ xu'$$

hence

$$inv(xu') = TRUE$$

which completes the proof.

The last three operations require no proof since they do not change the states and, therefore, are always valid. The complete specification of abstract data type Xusage is shown below.

```
ADT Xusage
  DOM Xusage = Module → Module-set;
  TYPE reaches: Module, Module, Xusage → Bool;
  AUX inv-Xusage(xu) ≜ U(rng xu) ⊆ dom xu;
  OPS
    INIT: →;
      post(-,xu') ≜ xu' = [];
    END INIT

    ADD_MOD: Module, Module-set →;
      pre(xu,mod,-) ≜ mod ∉ dom xu ∨ xu(mod) = {};
      post(xu,mod,uses,xu') ≜
          xu' = xu + [m ↦ {} : m ∈ (uses - dom xu)] † [mod ↦
                          uses];
    END ADD_MOD

    DEL_MOD: Module →;
      pre(xu,mod) ≜ mod ∈ dom xu;
      post(xu,mod,xu') ≜
          xu' = [m ↦ xu(m) - {mod} : m ∈ (dom xu - {mod})];
    END DEL_MOD

    USES: Module → Module-set;
      pre(xu,mod) ≜ mod ∈ dom xu;
      post(xu,mod,-,ms) ≜ ms = xu(mod);
    END USES

    USED_BY: Module → Module-set;
      pre(xu,mod) ≜ mod ∈ dom xu;
      post(xu,mod,-,ms) ≜ ms = {m : m ∈ dom xu ∧ mod ∈
                                    xu(m)};
    END USED_BY

    REC_MOD: → Module-set;
      post(xu,-,ms) ≜ ms = {m : m ∈ dom xu ∧
                              reaches(m,m,xu)};

      pre-reaches(m1,m2,xu) ≜ m1 ∈ dom xu ∧ m2 ∈ dom xu;
      reaches(m1,m2,xu) ≜ m2 ∈ xu(m1) ∨
                              (∃ m ∈ xu(m1): reaches(m,m2,xu));
    END REC_MOD
  END Xusage
```

6.2 Refinement of specification

Having completed the first specification of the system, the next stage involves refining the specification. First, we must choose a new, more concrete object class for the abstract data type. A number of possibilities exist; we suggest the following concrete object class

```
Xusage1 = Module → Cross;
Cross :: u: Module-set, b: Module-set;
```

Xusage1 is the domain of mappings from Module to a new domain called Cross. Every object in Cross has two components. The first component denotes the set of modules a module may use; the second component denotes the set of modules which may use that module. So, for example, the structure diagram in Figure 6.1 will be represented by the following mapping in Xusage1:

```
[mod1 ↦ ({mod2,mod3},{}),
 mod2 ↦ ({},{mod1}),
 mod3 ↦ ({},{mod1})]
```

What we have done, in fact, is introduced some redundancy in our model by explicitly including, for each module, the set of modules which may use that module. This is a **design decision**. The refinement process typically involves making one or more design decisions at each stage.

Every design decision must have some justification. The design decision above was made with the hope of gaining some conceptual efficiency in the system. We observe that the introduced redundancy may simplify some operations (e.g., USED_BY) at the cost of making other operations more complicated (e.g., ADD_MOD). In systems that deal with information storage and retrieval usually one requires the retrieve operations to be considerably simpler than the storage operations, for the simple reason that the former are used much more often than the latter. This is the basis of the design decision we have made here.

Our next task is to strengthen the data type invariant to preserve the meaning of the problem. The new data type invariant is:

```
inv-Xusage1(xu) ≙
    (∀ m ∈ dom xu: (∀ m1 ∈ xu(m).u: m ∈ xu(m1).b) ∧
                   (∀ m1 ∈ xu(m).b: m ∈ xu(m1).u) );
```

This simply states that the following must hold for every module m in the system: if m uses a module m1 then m should be in the set of modules that use m1 in the mapping, and that if m is used by a module m1 then m should be in the set of modules that m1 uses in the mapping. This is illustrated by Figure 6.3 for the system shown in Figure 6.1.

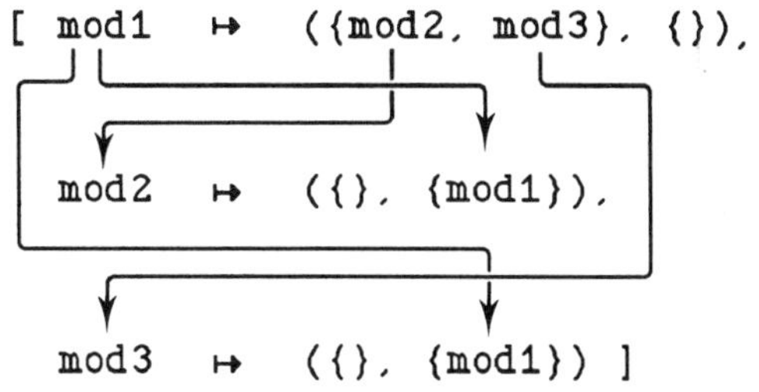

Figure 6.3 A diagrammatic view of *inv*-Xusage1.

The relationship between Xusage and Xusage1 is documented by the following retrieve function.

```
retr: Xusage1 → Xusage;
retr(xu1) ≙ [m ↦ xu1(m).u: m ∈ dom xu1];
```

We now show that retr is total over valid states and that Xusage1 is an adequate representation of Xusage.

Lemma 6.4
$$(\forall \; x1 \in Xusage1: \; inv\text{-}Xusage1(x1) \Rightarrow$$
$$(\exists \; x \in Xusage: \; x = retr(x1) \; \wedge \qquad\qquad (1)$$
$$inv\text{-}Xusage(retr(x1))))) \qquad\qquad (2)$$

Proof

(1) is immediate from the definition of retr. Consider (2), which is equivalent to showing that

$$\bigcup(rng \; x) \subseteq dom \; x$$

where

$$x = [m \mapsto x1(m).u: m \in dom \; x1] \qquad\qquad (3)$$

Using *inv*-Xusage1

$$\bigcup\{x1(m).u: m \in dom \; x1\} \subseteq dom \; x1$$

and, using (3), it reduces to

$$\bigcup(rng \; x) \subseteq dom \; x1$$

which completes the proof since using *inv*-Xusage1:

$$dom \ x1 \ = \ dom \ x \qquad\qquad\qquad\qquad \square$$

Lemma 6.5

Xusage1 is an adequate representation of Xusage.

Proof

Let $x \in$ Xusage and $inv\text{-}Xusage(x)$ = TRUE then

$$x1 \ = \ [m \ \mapsto \ mk\text{-}Cross(x(m),\{n: \ n \ \in \ dom \ x \ \wedge \ m \ \in \ x(n))) \ : \ m \ \in$$
$$dom \ x] \qquad\qquad\qquad\qquad\qquad (1)$$

represents x. To prove this, let $m \in$ dom $x1$, we must show that

$$(\forall \ m1 \ \in \ x1(m).u: \ m \ \in \ x1(m1).b) \qquad\qquad\qquad (2)$$

and that

$$(\forall \ m1 \ \in \ x1(m).b: \ m \ \in \ x1(m1).u) \qquad\qquad\qquad (3)$$

Using **(1)**, **(2)** reduces to

$$m1 \ \in \ x(m) \ \Rightarrow \ m \ \in \ \{n: \ n \ \in \ dom \ x \ \wedge \ m1 \ \in \ x(n)\}$$

which is immediate by considering the case n = m. Using **(1)** again, **(3)** reduces to

$$m1 \ \in \ \{n: \ n \ \in \ dom \ x \ \wedge \ m \ \in \ x(n)\} \ \Rightarrow \ m \ \in \ x(m1)$$

which is immediate by considering the case n = $m1$, and completes the proof. $\quad\square$

The next step in the refinement process involves producing operations in the representation which model the operations in the original specification. The first operation, INIT, will remain as before. Operation ADD_MOD is modelled by ADD_MOD1:

```
ADD_MOD1: Module, Module-set → ;
    pre(xu,mod,uses) ≙ mod ∉ dom xu ∨ xu(mod).u = {};
    post(xu,mod,uses,xu') ≙ xu' =
        xu † [m ↦ if m ∈ dom xu
                    then mk-Cross(xu(m).u,xu(m).b ∪ {mod})
                    else mk-Cross({},{mod}) : m ∈ uses]
                † [mod ↦ mk-Cross(uses,if mod ∈ dom xu
                                        then xu(mod).b else {})];
END ADD_MOD1
```

The pre-condition of ADD_MOD1 is more or less identical to that of ADD_MOD. The post-condition, however, has changed considerably. The explicit mapping in *post* produces the entry for mod itself. The implicit mapping produces an entry for each module in uses. It ensures that for each mapping m in uses, mod is included in the set xu'(m).b.

Let us now evaluate operation ADD_MOD1:

```
stat> VAR x: Xusage1;;
stat> INIT1(x);
stat> `x;
[]
stat> ADD_MOD1(x,"top",{"mid1","mid2"});
stat> ADD_MOD1(x,"mid1",{"mid1","bot1","bot2"});
*** post-state of ADD_MOD1 does not satisfy the
invariant
stat> `x;
["mid1" ↦ ({},{"top"}),
  "mid2" ↦ ({},{"top"}),
  "top" ↦ ({"mid2","mid1"},{})]
stat>
```

This simple evaluation shows that ADD_MOD1 does not preserve the data type invariant. Operation ADD_MOD1 is therefore not valid. If we examine the post-condition of this operation carefully we see that it does not behave properly when mod is recursive: if mod ∈ *dom* xu then

```
xu'(mod) = mk-Cross(uses,xu(m).b)
```

and if mod ∉ *dom* xu then

```
xu'(mod) = mk-Cross(uses,{})
```

Both cases produce wrong results since the second set will not contain mod. This problem is avoided by the following post-condition for ADD_MOD1.

```
post(xu,mod,uses,xu') ≙ xu' =
    xu † [m ↦ if m ∈ dom xu
            then mk-Cross(xu(m).u,xu(m).b ∪ {mod})
            else mk-Cross({},{mod}) : m ∈ uses]
        † [mod ↦ mk-Cross(uses,
            (if mod ∈ dom xu then xu(mod).b else {}) ∪
            (if mod ∈ uses then {mod} else {}))];
```

Let us now evaluate the new version of ADD_MOD1:

```
stat> VAR x: Xusage1;;
stat> INIT(x);
stat> `x;
[]
stat> ADD_MOD(x,"top",{"mid1","mid2"});
stat> ADD_MOD(x,"mid1",{"mid1","bot1","bot2"});
stat> ADD_MOD(x,"mid2",{"bot2"});
stat> ADD_MOD(x,"bot1",{"top","mid1"});
stat> `x;
["bot2"  ↦  ({},{"mid1","mid2"}),
  "mid2"  ↦  ({"bot2"},{"top"}),
  "top"   ↦  ({"mid2","mid1"},{"bot1"}),
  "mid1"  ↦
({"bot2","bot1","mid1"},{"top","mid1","bot1"}),
  "bot1"  ↦  ({"mid1","top"},{"mid1"})]
stat>
```

The behaviour is promising. Now we may attempt to prove that ADD_MOD1 preserves the data type invariant of Xusage1.

Lemma 6.6

ADD_MOD1 is valid.

Proof

We must show that:

$$pre(xu,mod,uses) \land inv(xu) \land post(xu,mod,uses,xu') \Rightarrow inv(xu')$$

Suppose that the left hand side of the implication is true. The proof then reduces to showing that for each module m in *dom* xu' the following are true:

$$(\forall\ m1 \in xu'(m).u:\ m \in xu'(m1).b) \tag{1}$$

and

$$(\forall\ m1 \in xu'(m).b:\ m \in xu'(m1).u) \tag{2}$$

Using *post*

$$(\forall\ m \in (dom\ xu - uses - \{mod\}):\ xu'(m) = xu(m)) \tag{3}$$

and

$$(\forall \; m \in (dom \; xu \; \cap \; uses): xu'(m).u = xu(m).u \; \wedge$$
$$xu'(m).b = xu(m).b \; \cup \; \{mod\}) \tag{4}$$

Now

$$(\forall \; m \in (dom \; xu \; \cap \; uses): m \in xu'(mod).u)$$
$$\Leftrightarrow (\forall \; m \in (dom \; xu \; \cap \; uses): m \in uses) \tag{5}$$

Using **(3)**,**(4)** and **(5)** the proof reduces to showing that **(1)** and **(2)** hold for any module m in uses $\cap$ {mod}. We shall consider two separate cases:

(i) Let m = mod, **(1)** then reduces to

$$(\forall \; m1 \in uses: m \in xu'(m1).b)$$

This is obvious and immediate from *post*. Consider **(2)**, the case when mod is recursive is obvious since (by *post*):

$$mod \in xu'(mod).b \; \wedge \; mod \in xu'(mod).u$$

So suppose mod is not recursive, i.e., mod $\notin$ uses. Two cases must be considered: when mod $\notin$ *dom* xu, by *post*:

$$xu'(mod).b = \{\}$$

hence **(2)** is immediate. When mod $\in$ *dom* xu, by *post*:

$$xu'(mod).b = xu(mod).b$$

So **(2)** reduces to

$$(\forall \; m1 \in xu(mod).b: m \in xu'(m1).u)$$

which is immediate from *inv-Xusage*, **(3)** and **(4)**.

(ii) Now consider uses - *dom* xu, we observe that (using *post*)

$$(\forall \; m \in (uses - dom \; xu - \{mod\}): xu'(m).u = \{\} \; \wedge$$
$$xu'(m).b = \{mod\})$$

hence **(1)** is immediate, and **(2)** reduces to

$$(\forall\ m\ \in\ (uses\ -\ dom\ xu\ -\ \{mod\}):\ (\forall\ m1\ \in\ \{mod\}:m\ \in\ xu'(m1).u))$$
$$\Leftrightarrow\ (\forall\ m\ \in\ (uses\ -\ dom\ xu\ -\ \{mod\}):\ m\ \in\ xu'(mod).u)$$
$$\Leftrightarrow\ (\forall\ m\ \in\ (uses\ -\ dom\ xu\ -\ \{mod\}:\ m\ \in\ uses)$$

which is immediate. □

Lemma 6.7

ADD_MOD1 models ADD_MOD.

Proof

We must show two things:

(i) We must show that given xu1 ∈ Xusage1 then

$$inv\text{-}Xusage1(xu1)\ \wedge\ pre\text{-}ADD\_MOD(retr(xu1),mod,uses)$$
$$\Rightarrow\ pre\text{-}ADD\_MOD1(xu1,mod,uses)$$

Suppose that the left hand side of the implication is true, and let:

$$xu\ =\ retr(xu1)\ =\ [m\ \mapsto\ xu1(m).u:\ m\ \in\ dom\ xu1] \tag{1}$$

Using *pre*-ADD_MOD:

$$mod\ \notin\ dom\ xu\ \vee\ xu(mod)\ =\ \{\}$$

Using **(1)** this reduces to

$$mod\ \notin\ dom\ xu1\ \vee\ xu1(mod).u\ =\ \{\}$$

which verifies the right hand side of the implication.

(ii) Given that xu1 ∈ Xusage1 we must show that:

$$inv\text{-}Xusage1(xu1)\ \wedge\ pre\text{-}ADD\_MOD1(xu1,mod,uses)\ \wedge$$
$$post\text{-}ADD\_MOD1(xu1,mod,uses,xu1')$$
$$\Rightarrow post\text{-}ADD\_MOD(retr(xu1),mod,uses,retr(xu1'))$$

Suppose that the left hand side of the implication is true. It is easy to show that retr is distributive over †, i.e.,

$$retr(m1\ \dagger\ m2)\ =\ retr(m1)\ \dagger\ retr(m2)$$

for any two mappings m1 and m2 in Xusage1. Applying retr to *post*-ADD_MOD1 we get

```
      retr(xu1')
  = retr(xu1) † retr[m ↦ if m ∈ dom xu1
                           then mk-Cross(xu1(m).u, ...)
                           else mk-Cross({}, ...) : m ∈ uses]
               † retr[mod ↦ mk-Cross(uses, ...)]
  = retr(xu1) † [m ↦ if m ∈ dom retr(xu1)
                        then xu1(m).u else {} : m ∈ uses]
               † [mod ↦ uses]
  = retr(xu1) † [m ↦ xu1(m).u: m ∈ (uses ∩ dom retr(xu1))]
               † [m ↦ {}: m (uses - dom retr(xu1))] † [mod ↦
                                                          uses]
  = (retr(xu1) † [m ↦ retr(xu1(m)) : m ∈ (uses ∩ dom
                                              retr(xu1))])
    † [m ↦ {}: m ∈ (uses - dom retr(xu1))]
    † [mod ↦ uses]
  = retr(xu1) † [m ∈ {}: m ∈ (uses - dom retr(xu1))]
               † [mod ↦ uses]
```

which verifies the right hand side of the implication and completes the proof.   □

From the above lemmas it follows that operation ADD_MOD1 is correct and models ADD_MOD. The refinement, evaluation and verification of other operations is very similar to ADD_MOD and is not further discussed here. The complete specification of Xusage1 is given below.

ADT Xusage1

```
  DOM Xusage1 = Module → Cross;
      Cross :: u: Module-set, b: Module-set;
  TYPE reaches: Module, Module, Xusage1 → Bool;

  AUX inv-Xusage1(xu) ≙
          (∀ m ∈ dom xu: (∀ m1 ∈ xu(m).u: m ∈ xu(m1).b) ∧
                          (∀ m1 ∈ xu(m).b: m ∈ xu(m1).u));
  OPS
    INIT1: → ;
        post(-,xu') ≙ xu' = [];
    END INIT1

    ADD_MOD1: Module, Module-set → ;
        pre(xu,mod,uses) ≙ mod ∉ dom xu ∨ xu(mod).u = {};
        post(xu,mod,uses,xu') ≙ xu' = xu
            † [m ↦ if m ∈ dom xu
                    then mk-Cross(xu(m).u,xu(m).b ∪ {mod})
```

```
                        else mk-Cross({},{mod}) : m ∈ uses]
          † [mod ↦ mk-Cross(uses,
                        (if mod ∈ dom xu then xu(mod).b else {}) ∪
                        (if mod ∈ uses then {mod} else {}))];
     END ADD_MOD1

     DEL_MOD1: Module → ;
        pre(xu,mod) ≙ mod ∈ dom xu;
        post(xu,mod,xu') ≙
            xu' = [m ↦ mk-Cross(xu(m).u - {mod}, xu(m).b - {mod})
                        : m ∈ (dom xu - {mod})];
     END DEL_MOD1

     USES1: Module → Module-set;
        pre(xu,mod) ≙ mod ∈ dom xu;
        post(xu,mod,-,ms) ≙ ms = xu(mod).u;
     END USES1

     USED_BY1: Module → Module-set;
        pre(xu,mod) ≙ mod ∈ dom xu;
        post(xu,mod,-,ms) ≙ ms = xu(mod).b;
     END USED_BY1

     REC_MOD1: → Module-set;
        post(xu,-,ms) ≙ ms = {m : m ∈ dom xu ∧ reaches(m,m,xu)};
        pre-reaches(m1,m2,xu) ≙ m1 ∈ dom xu ∧ m2 ∈ dom xu;
        reaches(m1,m2,xu) ≙ m2 ∈ xu(m1).u ∨
                            (∃ m ∈ xu(m1).u: reaches(m,m2,xu));
     END REC_MOD1
END Xusage1
```

6.3 Discussion

By borrowing ideas from the Vienna Development Method (VDM), we have arrived at a notation that, while preserving the useful features of VDM, such as conciseness and formality, lends itself to execution.

The provision of an abstract data type encapsulation mechanism on top of VDM has enabled us to formulate a software system specification at different levels of abstraction more easily. Two advantages are gained here. First, the encapsulation enables us to enforce useful disciplines, e.g., that an abstract data type is manipulated through its own set of private operations only. Second, it allows us to talk about abstract data types as objects, both conceptually and in reality. This in turn facilitates the construction of formal specification libraries which consist of self-contained abstract data type specifications. Libraries of this form would be an indispensable tool in software development and prototyping: they significantly reduce the verification effort by allowing developers to build on top of each other's work. Once an abstract data type is developed, verified and deposited in the library, subsequent users can employ it and rely on its correctness. This is, of course, the familiar reusable software approach to prototyping, but it is more productive since it is applied to a higher, more stable level of abstraction.

Needless to say, by requiring our notation to be executable, we have necessitated some compromises concerning the implicitness of EPROL. For example, the implicit predicate

$$(\exists\ x\ \in\ Real:\ x*x\ -\ x\ =\ 2)$$

is not executable in EPROL since the search domain is potentially infinite. The implication of this is that certain styles of VDM predicates, while expressible in EPROL, are not executable. This does not necessarily mean that we have to restrict ourselves to executable constructs. Indeed, in our developments, we first produce a specification using any construct that we find appropriate. Once a specification is produced in this way, its transformation to an executable form is straightforward and involves very little effort.

The essential difference between the VDM approach and our approach is in the priorities these two assign to different aspects of development. VDM primarily concerns itself with rigorous verification of correctness from the start. EPROS regards verification as a complementary option. It primarily concerns itself with the appropriateness of a specification and with experimenting with alternative designs, and argues that executing a specification before verification can detect errors more easily and at a greatly reduced cost. This opinion is also shared by a number of other researchers [Goguen 1984, Kemmerer 1985, Henderson 1986].

6.4 Summary

This chapter has shown how the functionality of a simple system can be expressed using the facilities of VDM. Furthermore, it has demonstrated how EPROS can be used to prototype such a system. Used in conjunction with mathematical verification such prototyping is capable of producing a system with a high degree of correctness and which matches user requirements.

Chapter 7
Implementation

This chapter describes the implementation notation of EPROL. It introduces various implementation constructs and the most basic facility for modularization – imperative functions. Functions may be used for concrete realization of several abstractions, e.g. abstract data types. Other forms of modules will be described in the next two chapters.

The implementation notation is not isolated from the specification notation. In fact, all the constructs and objects described in Chapter 5 (e.g. combinators and sets) can be used freely in the implementation notation.

7.1 Statements

In the implementation notation, computation is usually defined in terms of statements. These are computation rules that cause useful side-effects.

7.1.1 Assignment

This is the most elementary form of statement, the general form for which is:

```
location := expression
```

The effect of this statement is that expression is first evaluated and the resulting value is stored in location. Examples are

```
x := 12**3;
ll := <<"x">,<"y","z">>;
m("John") := 30;
t.r := [1->1, 2->4];
```

where x is an integer, ll is a list, m is a mapping and t is a tree variable.

7.1.2 Control structures

The simplest form of control statement is the if-then-else statement. It may take one of the following two forms.

```
if bool_expr then
     stat1;

if bool_expr then
     stat1
else
     stat2;
```

In both cases bool_expr is evaluated first. If it evaluates to TRUE then stat1 is executed. If it evaluates to FALSE then in the former case nothing will happen whereas in the latter case stat2 will be executed.

There are two kinds of multi-branch control statements. The first is the mac statement; this is very similar to the mac expression and has the general form.

```
mac {
     bool_expr1 → stat1;
     bool_expr2 → stat2;
     :
     bool_exprn → statn;
};
```

where the expressions bool_expr on the left hand side are evaluated in the order they appear. If bool_expri evaluates to TRUE then stati will be executed and the mac statement will terminate.

The second multi-branch statement is the cases statement; this is very similar to the cases expression and has the general form.

```
cases exprs {
    expr1 → stat1;
    expr2 → stat2;
    :
    exprn → statn;
};
```

where exprs is evaluated first and then the expressions expri are evaluated in the order they appear. If expri = exprs then stati will be executed and the cases statement will terminate.

7.1.3   Loop structures

Three kinds of loop structure are provided. The for-do statement iterates over the elements of a set or a list. It has the general form

```
for var in expr do
    stat;
```

where var is a bound variable and expr is a set or list expression. The bound variable needs no declaration. This statement iterates var over individual objects in expr. If expr is a set expression then iteration will be done pseudo nondeterministically.

The while-do statement executes a statement repeatedly while a predicate is true, and has the general form:

```
while bool_expr do
    stat;
```

It evaluates the bool_expr first; if it evaluates to TRUE then it will execute stat. This process is repeated until bool_expr evaluates to FALSE at which time the loop is terminated.

The do-while statement executes a statement repeatedly until a predicate becomes false, and has the general form:

```
do
    stat;
while bool_expr;
```

Here stat is first executed, then bool_expr is evaluated. If it evaluates to TRUE then the whole process is repeated again, otherwise the loop is terminated.

Two other related statements are the done and the goto statement. The former appears in a loop structure and when executed terminates the loop immediately. The latter is used for explicit jump to a statement within a sequence of statements.

7.1.4   Blocks

A sequence of statements may be grouped together to form a block by enclosing them within curly brackets, i.e.:

```
{ stat1;
    stat2;
    :
    statn;
}
```

A block is itself treated as a single statement.

7.1.5   Assertions

Recording important invariants when writing programs is a good practice. In EPROL such invariants may be specified using assertion statements. An assertion statement has the general form:

```
assert(bool_expr);
```

When this statement is executed the bool_expr is evaluated; if it evaluates to TRUE then nothing will happen, otherwise the system will report that the assertion has failed. For example, the statement

```
assert(∀ i ∈ {1:len l - 1}: l[i] ⩽ l[i+1]);
```

asserts that a list of numbers l is sorted in ascending order.

7.2   Data types

The data types described in Chapter 5 (i.e., elementary types such as integers, and composite types such as sets) can be used directly in the implementation notation.

In particular, trees may be used to implement record structures. Also, any abstract data types defined by the programmer in the specification part can be used freely.

Except for the elementary types, objects of all other types are dynamic. EPROL uses a heap storage mechanism for storing these objects, which is automatically garbage collected.

Certain additional data types are also provided, the use of which is restricted to the implementation part. These are briefly described below.

7.2.1   Arrays

An array is a composite object of predefined length, containing a contiguous sequence of objects of the same type. For example,

    array[5] *Int*

defines an array of five integers. Arrays may be one or multi-dimensional. In general, an array type has the form

    array[e1][e2]...[en] Elem

where e1,e2,...,en are arbitrary positive integer expressions, and Elem is the type of array elements. Arrays may also be dynamic, i.e., their size may be decided at run time. Array elements are referenced in a manner identical to lists, albeit the index starts at 0.

7.2.2   Files

A file refers to an external storage space; file is supported by a predefined type denoted by the keyword file. File operations are described in Appendix A.

7.2.3   Forms

Electronic forms are special abstract data types in EPROL (see Chapter 8). A form type is defined as: *form* form_id, where form_id is the name of a form module. Form operations are described in Appendix A.

7.2.4   Databases

The term database in EPROL refers to a collection of records which are stored and retrieved by a key. Every record in a database must be either a form image or a tree branch. For example, Student defines a database domain called St_dbase where every record in such a database is an element of Student.

```
DOM Student :: name: Str, age: Nat, sub: Str;
    St_dbase = Student-dbase(key=name);
```

These records are stored by the name key. Similarly,

```
DOM Ap_dbase = (form Appliance_order)-dbase(key=$code);
```

defines a form database domain. Database operations are described in Appendix A.

7.3   Input and output

Input and output can be performed with respect to standard channels, external channels, and windows. All such I/O is formatted. In addition, composite objects can be pretty printed using a special output function.

7.3.1   Ordinary I/O

Standard and external formatted I/O is primarily supported by two functions called put and get. Put sends its output to either the standard output or an external file. It has the following call form

```
put(file, format, arg1, ..., argn);
```

where file is optional and indicates the destination of output, and format is a string which contains the output format specifications for arg1, ..., argn. The format specifications follow the conventions of C [Kernighan and Ritchie 1978].

Get obtains its input from either the standard input or an external file. The general call form for get is

```
get(file, string, loc1, ..., locn);
```

where file and string are optional. Get first outputs string (if any and if file is not present) and then reads n values and stores them in locations loc1, ..., locn.

7.3.2   Window-oriented I/O

EPROL supports the creation and manipulation of overlapping windows. Windows can be treated as channels for sending output and receiving input. Window functions and I/O operations are described in Appendix A. An example of a window function is given below.

```
w_text(6,43,"^RText Frame^N",
        \In EPROL printing mode is controlled by ^^
                ^^N     prints in Normal mode
                ^^B     prints in ^BBold^N mode
                ^^U     prints in ^UUnderline^N mode
                ^^K     prints in ^KblinK^N mode
                ^^R     prints in ^RReverse video^N mode\);
```

It creates the following window.

```
┌─Text Frame───────────────────────────────────┐
│ In EPROL printing mode is controlled by ^     │
│     ^N      prints in Normal mode             │
│     ^B      prints in Bold mode               │
│     ^U      prints in Underline mode          │
│     ^K      prints in blinK mode              │
│     ^R      prints in Reverse video mode      │
└───────────────────────────────────────────────┘
```

7.3.3   Pretty printing

The function ppr is responsible for pretty printing objects in EPROL and is extensively used by the interpreter. It takes an expression as argument and pretty prints its value. For example,

```
ppr(power{"apple","orange","pear"});
```

will produce:

```
{{},
 {"pear"},
 {"pear","orange"},
 {"orange"},
 {"pear","apple"},
 {"pear","orange","apple"},
 {"orange","apple"}
 {"apple"}}
```

7.4 Imperative functions

Imperative functions are defined by the FUNCTION module; they correspond to procedures and functions in modern programming languages and support procedural abstraction. Figure 7.1 shows the general structure of a FUNCTION module.

The parameter list and/or result type may be empty. It specifies the names and domains of function parameters. Each parameter is specified as the following extract

```
par : dom
```

if it is a value parameter, or as

```
VAR par : dom
```

if it is a variable parameter. The DOM part of a function is similar to the DOM part of an abstract data type. The VAR part defines one or more variables. For example, the declaration

```
VAR 1: Int-list := <1,10,100>;
```

defines 1 to be a list of integers and initialize 1 to <1,10,100>.

```
FUNCTION  ifun_id (... parameter-list ...): result_type;
DOM  ... private domain definitions ...
VAR  ... private variable definitions ...
          :
       local definitions
          :
BEGIN
        :
      statements
        :
END ifun_id
```

Figure 7.1 The general structure of a FUNCTION module.

The body of a function consists of a sequence of statements. A function can also contain local FUNCTION, DIALOGUE, FORM and CLUSTER modules. An example of a function module is shown in Figure 7.2. It is an implementation of the familiar quick sort algorithm.

```
FUNCTION quick_sort(table: Table, size: Nat);
DOM Table = array[size] Str;
   FUNCTION quick_sort_aux(lower:Nat0, upper:Nat0);
   VAR i:  Nat0 := lower;
       j:  Nat0 := upper;
       key: Str := table[(lower+upper)/2];
     FUNCTION swap(VAR x: *, VAR y: *);
     VAR temp: *;
     BEGIN
         temp := x;
         x := y;
         y := temp;
     END swap
   BEGIN
       do {
           while table[j].name > key do j := j - 1;
           while table[i].name < key do i := i + 1;
           if i <= j then {
               swap(table[i],table[j]);
               i := i + 1;
               j := j - 1;
           };
       }
   while i ⩽ j;
       if i < upper then quick_sort_aux(i,upper);
       if lower < j then quick_sort_aux(lower,j);
   END quick_sort_aux
BEGIN
    quick_sort_aux(0,size-1);
END quick_sort
```

Figure 7.2 A quicksort algorithm expressed in EPROL.

7.5 Summary

This chapter has described the programming facilities of EPROL. These facilities are very similar to those provided in languages such as Pascal and C and include statements, arrays, functions and files. The structure of an EPROL program is also similar to those of conventional languages which use a block-structured paradigm.

Chapter 8
User Interfaces

This chapter describes the notation of EPROL for user interface specification and development. This notation consists of an encapsulation mechanism for separating dialogues from functionality and a number of independent abstractions supporting well-developed concepts in user interfaces. Unlike functional specifications, the dialogue specification notation is initially graphical and semi-formal; the details of this notation are described below.

8.1 State transition diagrams

The state transition diagram (STD) notation employed by EPROL is based on the one proposed by Denert [1977]. This is an extension of the usual STD notation and allows one to describe dialogue systems hierarchically. The symbols used in this notation are summarized in Figure 8.1. Each symbol which describes a state is briefly described below.

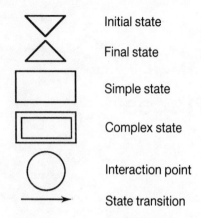

Figure 8.1 State transition diagram symbols.

- **Initial state** – Denotes the entry point for an STD. An STD must have exactly one initial state.

- **Final state** – Denotes the exit point for an STD. An STD must have exactly one final state.

- **Simple state** – Represents an action which involves no interaction with the user and is executed immediately. The action is usually described by a brief text in the box.

- **Complex state** – Is an abstraction of an entire STD which may be refined separately. A complex state may involve interaction with the user; for this reason, the system may remain in a complex state for an arbitrary length of time. A complex state may be labelled by a brief description of its function for readability.

- **Interaction point** – Denotes a state in which actual interaction between the user and the computer takes place. Interaction points are usually labelled by a number or abbreviation.

- **State transition** – Indicates transition between states. Arrows entering and emerging from a complex state are conceptually tied to the initial and final states of the refinement of that state, respectively. An arrow emerging from an interaction point must be labelled with user input or a predicate which will trigger that transition.

Complex states allow the abstraction of an entire STD in much the same way functions allow the abstraction of a sequence of processing steps. Using this notation, dialogue systems may be modularized and designed in a top-down manner.

8.1.1 The DIALOGUE module

Once a dialogue system is specified as an STD it is then converted to the one dimensional notation of EPROL. This notation is supported by the DIALOGUE module. The general structure of a DIALOGUE module is shown in Figure 8.2.

A DIALOGUE module represents a complex state. Each part of a DIALOGUE module is the same as that of a FUNCTION module except for the body. The body consists of one or more state descriptions where each state is either a simple state or an interaction point. A simple state has the form

```
state state_id1: action → state_id2;
```

where action is a statement. It defines a simple state called state_id1 which performs the specified action and then moves to state_id2. State_id2 itself must be a simple state or interaction point in the same DIALOGUE module. An interaction point has the form

```
DIALOGUE dial_id(...parameter-list...) : result-type
D O M...private domain definitions ...
VAR ...private variable definitions ...
       :
     local definitions
       :
BEGIN
        :
       state descriptions
        :
END   dial_id
```

Figure 8.2 The general structure of a DIALOGUE module.

```
iap stat_id: input_action;
    : pred1, output_action1 → stat_id1;
    : pred2, output_action2 → stat_id2;
    : pred3                 → stat_id3;
    : ....
    : ....
    : TRUE                  → stat_idn;
```

where `input_action` and `output_actions` are all statements. Each `stat_idi` must be a simple state or interaction point in the same `DIALOGUE` module. Each predicate `predi` is a predicate over user input or program variables. As shown above, `output_actions` are optional. Also, the last predicate may be simply TRUE, specifying a transition which will take place if no other predicate evaluates to TRUE. The above description defines an interaction point called `stat_id`. In this state, first `input_action` is performed; then the predicates are evaluated in the order they occur. If `predi` evaluates to TRUE then `output_actioni` will be performed (if any) and the system will move to `stat_idi`. An `iap` description must specify at least one state transition.

The first state in a `DIALOGUE` body is assumed to be the initial state. The final state is defined implicitly using `return` statements. For example, in

```
state s1: action → return(10);
```

`action` is first executed and then the `DIALOGUE` module is terminated, returning the number 10. All such `return` statements are conceptually tied to the `DIALOGUE` module's final state.

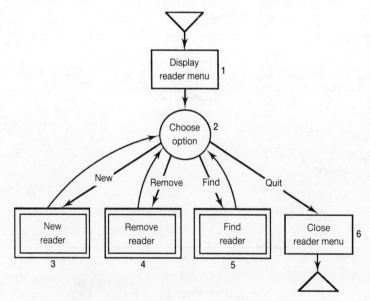

Figure 8.3 A simple state transition diagram.

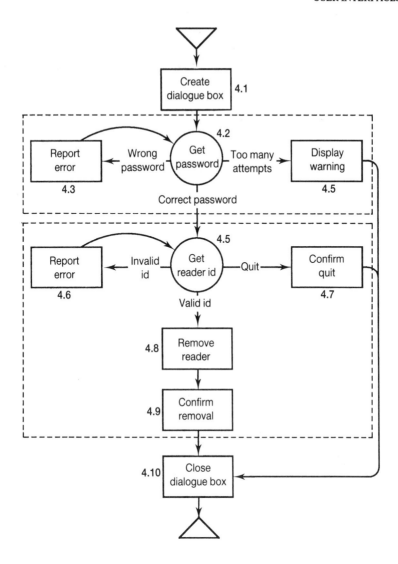

Figure 8.4 Refinement of complex state 'remove reader'.

8.1.2 An example

This section will illustrate, by means of an example, the way in which a simple dialogue may be specified as an STD and then implemented by a DIALOGUE module. Figure 8.3 shows an STD which is part of the user interface specification of a library system (see Chapter 10). The STD contains three complex states. A refinement of the complex state remove reader is shown in Figure 8.4. The refinement is at the bottom of the dialogue hierarchy since it contains no further complex states.

The first state in the refinement is a simple state which creates a dialogue box within which all subsequent interaction will take place. The STD then moves to an interaction point which asks the user for a password. If the user types a wrong password the STD will move to state 4.3, report the error and move back to the interaction point. If the user makes too many wrong guesses the STD will move to state 4.5, warn the user that further interaction is denied and then move to state 4.10. When a correct password is given the STD will move to interaction point 4.5 where the user is asked for the id of the reader who is to be removed. Invalid ids are handled by the simple state 4.6. Instead of giving an id, the user may quit the dialogue, in which case the STD will move to state 4.7, confirm the quit and then move to state 4.10. However, if the user supplies a valid id., the STD will move to state 4.8 and then 4.9, where it will remove the specified reader and confirm the removal respectively. The STD will then move to state 4.10 where the dialogue box is closed, and lastly to the final state.

The STD in Figure 8.4 can be directly implemented by a DIALOGUE module. However, before implementation, one should always look for potential simplifications in the diagram. Typically, many simple states can be squeezed into their neighbouring interaction points. In this way one can reduce the number of states in a DIALOGUE module considerably and hence simplify the implementation. The two boxes with dashed lines in Figure 8.4 depict this point.

The first box, for example, suggests that simple states 4.3 and 4.5 can be squeezed into interaction point 4.2. This practice is referred to as **state reduction**. An implementation of the STD, using the suggested state reductions, is given below. It consists of four states. Simple state box corresponds to state 4.1 in Figure 8.4. The assertion in this state ensures that the user has permission to do a removal operation. The function message displays a note or warning at the bottom of the dialogue box. Interaction point pass corresponds to state 4.2 and its associated simple states. Interaction point read corresponds to state 4.5 and its associated simple states. The last state, out, is a simple state and corresponds to state 4.10.

```
DIALOGUE  remove_reader(VAR  rmv_list:  Id-list,  VAR  rmv_ok:
Bool);
VAR width:    Nat := 30;
    passwd:   Str;
    attempts: Nat0 := 0;
    id:       Id;
BEGIN
    state box: { assert(rmv_ok);
                 w_open(3,width, "^M Remove Reader ^N");
                 message(3,NOTE,"");
               }                                    → pass;
    iap pass: { w_move(1,1);
                w_get(" Password:  ",passwd,8,noecho);
                message(3,NOTE,"");
              };
```

```
┌─Remove Reader────────────────────┐
│ Password:    _____            │
│ Reader Id:   3460__              │
│ Removed                          │
└──────────────────────────────────┘
```

Figure 8.5 The dialogue box for removing a reader.

```
      : passwd = DEL_PASS                  → read;
      : attempts ⩾ ATTEMPT_LIM,
              { message(3,WARN,"Imposter!");
                rmv_ok := FALSE;
                wait(2);
              }                                → out;
        : TRUE, { attempts := attempts+1;
                    message(3,WARN,"Wrong!");
                  }                            → pass;
  iap read: { w_move(2,1);
              w_get(" Reader Id: ",id,5)
            };
        : db_find(rds_db,id) ≠ NIL,
          { rmv_list := rmv_list ⌢ <id>;
            message(3,NOTE,"Removed");
          }                                      → out;
        : id = 0, message(3,NOTE,"Quited")       → out;
        : TRUE,   message(3,WARN,"Non-existant!") → read;
  state out: w_close(1)  → return;
END remove_reader
```

Figure 8.5 shows the effect of the dialogue on the screen. It shows the dialogue box after a reader has been successfully removed.

8.2   Pop-up menus

Many modern interactive systems are menu driven [Smith *et al.* 1982, Webster and Miner 1983]. In such systems the user interface usually consists of a network of menus where each menu serves a particular task. The user sends his request to the system by moving to the relevant menu and then selecting the required option.

Menus can be broadly classified into two categories. Each option of a menu in the first category denotes an action. Each option of a menu in the second category corresponds to a binary switch, i.e., it is either on or off. These two categories are supported by the menu and switch statements in EPROL, respectively. Each is briefly described below.

8.2.1   The menu statement

A menu specification consists of the following.

- A menu title.
- A set of option names.
- A set of constraints where each option may be associated with, at most, one constraint. A constraint will indicate, at any point in time, whether an option is active. Options with no constraint are always active. Only active options may be selected by the user. The set of active options is called the **active set**.
- A set of actions where each option must be associated with one action.

Menus are specified by the menu statement; this has the general form

```
menu {
    title
    option1, constraint pred1 → action1;
    option2                   → action2;
    :
    :
    optionk, constraint predk → actionk;
};
```

where title and options are all strings, preds are Boolean expressions and actions are arbitrary statements. Options 1 and k above are both constrained; the second option is unconstrained.

As an example, consider a menu which allows the user to do insert, delete, and change operations on the records of a database. The menu specification will look something like

```
menu {
    "^RDB-operation^N"
    "Insert record", constraint size < MAX_SIZE → ins_rec();
    "Change record", constraint size > 0        → chg_rec();
    "Delete record", constraint size > 0        → del_rec();
    "Help" → menu {
                "^RHelp^N"
                "Insert" →  ...;
```

```
            "Change"  →  ...;
            "Delete"  →  ...;
            "Back to last menu" → exit;
      };
};
```

where modules `ins_rec`, `chg_rec` and `del_rec` deal with insertion, change and deletion of records and are not further specified here. The variable `size` denotes the number of records in the database. `MAX_SIZE` is an upper bound on the size of the database. The last option in the menu is unconstrained. The action associated with this option is itself a `menu` statement which provides help for operations in the original menu. The help texts are not specified here. The word `exit` in the last option of the help menu specifies that when this option is selected the help menu will be closed and control will be sent back to the original menu.

Figure 8.6a shows what the menu will look like on the screen when actually activated. As shown in the figure, active options (i.e., 1 and 4) appear in bold. The option the user is at (i.e., option 4) is always highlighted. The system ensures that the user will not be able to select inactive options. The user can move from the

Figure 8.6a Menu as seen on the screen.

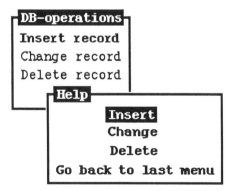

Figure 8.6b The help option is itself a menu.

current option to the previous/next option by pressing the arrow keys, and select an option by pressing the return key.

Figure 8.6b shows the effect of selecting the last option. A further menu is opened, giving the options on which help is available.

8.2.2 The switch statement

A switch specification consists of the following.

* A switch title.
* A set of option names.
* A set of constraints as in a menu.
* A predicate per option. If this predicate evaluates to TRUE then the option will be set, otherwise it will be reset.
* An action per option. The action is executed whenever the corresponding option is selected.

A switch statement takes the general form

```
switch {
    title
    option1, constraint cons1, tick pred1 → action1;
    option2,                    tick pred2 → action2;
                :
                :
    optionk, constraint consk, tick predk → actionk;
};
```

where constraints have the same role as they had in menus and are optional. Each option must be associated with a tick predicate. If this predicate evaluates to TRUE then the option will be ticked (i.e., marked on the left hand side to show that it is set). Like a menu, each switch option is associated with an action. When optioni is selected actioni will be executed.

To give an example, suppose we wish to allow the user to control the following parameters in a dialogue.

* verbose   whether the system response should be brief or verbose.
* warnings   whether the system should give warnings when it finds it appropriate to do so.
* prompt   whether the dialogue prompt should be displayed or hidden.

- **cursor**   whether the cursor should appear as a block or an underscore.

- **tabs**   whether the system should convert tabs into spaces.

Each of these may be represented by a Boolean variable, for example:

```
VAR verb, warn, prompt,
    blockcursor, convtabs: Bool := FALSE;
```

The facility may then be provided by a switch statement:

```
switch {
    "^RModes^N",
    "verbose",        constraint level>1, tick verb →
                                  verb := ¬verb;
    "give warnings", tick verb ∨ warn   → warn := ¬warn ∨ verb;
    "give prompt",   tick verb ∨ prompt →
                                  prompt:= ¬prompt ∨ verb;
    "block cursor", tick blockcursor   →
                                  blockcursor := ¬blockcursor;
    "convert tabs", tick convtabs      → convtabs := ¬convtabs;
};
```

The variable level denotes the level of the dialogue. So, as specified in the first option, the user may only choose the verbose mode when he is at some level other than the first. The action for this option simply toggles the variable verb. The next two options are dependent on the first option, in the sense that when the dialogue is in the verbose mode the warning and prompt modes will be set anyway. This is ensured by including verb as a disjunction in the tick predicates of the second and third options.

Initially, the switch frame will appear on the screen as shown in Figure 8.7a. If the user, for example, selects the first option the first three options will be ticked, as shown in Figure 8.7b. If the user again selects the first option the first three options will be reset taking us back to Figure 8.7a.

Figure 8.7a A switch frame.

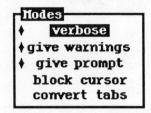

Figure 8.7b Switch frame after the first option is selected.

8.3   Electronic forms

A useful concept in user interface design is electronic forms. These are commonly used in office automation systems and are exceptionally suitable for changeover from manual to computer-based systems [Tsichritzis 1980, Yao *et al.* 1984]. The most useful aspect of forms is that they reflect the logical relationship between data items in a user interface [Tsichritzis 1982, Gehani 1982b].

8.3.1   The form module

The EPROL notation for defining electronic forms is based on the notation proposed by Gehani [1983] who suggested that forms should be specified as abstract data types. Forms are defined using the FORM module, the general structure of which is shown in Figure 8.8.

```
FORM form_id;
   \...................
   .. form layout ...
   ...................\
   :
 field definitions
   :
 END form_id
```

Figure 8.8 The general structure of a FORM module.

The form layout part defines the layout of the form as it will appear on the screen. A form is always displayed in a window. The two backslash characters in the form layout denote the top left hand corner and the bottom right hand corner of the window. In a form layout, each field appears as a field identifier. This is just like a normal identifier, preceded by a $ symbol (e.g., $name).

Each field that appears in the layout part must be defined in the field definitions part. Each field is defined by specifying its type, maximum size, and optionally one or more attributes. The attributes define the properties of the field. An attribute may be any of the following.

•	after	specifies that the field must be filled after certain other fields.
•	computed	gives a computation rule (a statement) that the system will use to compute the field automatically.
•	constraint	imposes a constraint that must be satisfied when the field is filled. If the constraint fails user data will be rejected.
•	initially	defines an initial value for the field. The field will maintain this value unless the user changes it during interaction.
•	lock	specifies one or more fields which will be locked after the field is filled.
•	noecho	specifies that the user data for the field must not be echoed on the screen (e.g., a password).
•	optional	specifies that the field is optional and may be filled if the user wishes to do so.
•	permanent	specifies that the field is permanent, i.e., once filled it may not be changed.
•	required	specifies that a value for the field is required and must be supplied by the user. This is the default case.
•	system	specifies that the field will be automatically filled by the system.

8.3.2   An example

To illustrate the use of the FORM module, consider the following form definition; it defines a form called appliance_order. Everything in the form layout, apart from the field identifiers, is treated literally. Escape sequences are understood here too; for example, Appliance and Customer are both specified to be printed in bold.

In the field definition part, a field is typically defined to be of type Int, Real or Str. The first field, for example, is defined to be of type Str, having a maximum length of 12 characters. This field is also defined to be required. The second field has a lock attribute; it specifies that when it is filled the $name field will be locked. The third field specifies, by means of a constraint attribute, that $quantity must be an integer between 0 and 100. The fifth field is computed automatically; here, an after attribute is used to ensure that all variables used in the computation are already bound. The last field is filled automatically by the system; the identifier sdate here stands for short date (e.g., 12/02/86).

```
FORM appliance_order;
  \^BAppliance:^N
      Name:       $name                   Code:      $code
      Quantity:   $quantity               Price:     $price
                                    Total Price:     $totprice

  ^BCustomer^N
      Name:       $cname
      Address:    $street
                  $town
                  $county
      Post Code: $postcode            Delivery: $delivery

      Department: $dept                     Date: $date          \
  $name:      Str (12), required;     /* required is the
                                          default */
  $code:      Int (5), lock ($name);
  $quantity: Int (5), constraint 0 < $quantity < 100;
  $price:     Real (6), after ($name,$code);
  $totprice: Real (8), after ($quantity,$price),
              computed $totprice := $quantity*$price;
  $cname:     Str (14);
  $street:    Str (24);
  $town:      Str (24);
  $county:    Str (24);
  $postcode: Str (7), optional;
  $delivery: Str (4), after ($code),
              computed menu {
                      "By Post"              → $delivery := "POST";
                      "By Ship"              → $delivery := "SHIP";
                      "Special Delivery", constraint $code<1000,
                                          → $delivery := "SDEL";
                      "To Be Collected" → $delivery := "TBC";
                      };
  $dept:      Str (12);
  $date:      Str (8), system (sdate);
END appliance_order
```

Figure 8.9a shows what the form will look like on the screen when activated. As shown there, the position of the fields directly conforms to that specified by the form layout part. Figure 8.9b shows the form when the user is actually filling the

```
┌Appliance Order Form─────────────────────────────────────┐
│ Appliance                                                │
│    Name:        _____        Code:      _____     │
│    Quantity:      _____            Price:     _____      │
│                              Total Price:    _____     │
│                                                          │
│ Customer                                                 │
│    Name:        _____                             │
│    Address:       _____               │
│                   _____               │
│                   _____               │
│    Post Code:   _____        Delivery:  ____           │
│                                                          │
│ Department:   _____        Date:  _____         │
└──────────────────────────────────────────────────────────┘
```

Figure 8.9a Form as seen on the screen.

```
┌Appliance Order Form─────────────────────────────────────┐
│ Appliance                                                │
│    Name:     Freezer_____        Code:    01233         │
│    Quantity: 2____                Price:   452.00        │
│                              Total Price:  904.00__      │
│                                                          │
│ Customer                                                 │
│    Name:     J. Green_____                              │
│    Address:  5, Commercial Road_____                    │
│              Seaford_____                     │
│              East Sussex_____                     │
│    Post Code: SF2 4QR              Delivery ┌Delivery┐   │
│                                             │ By Post │  │
│ Department:   _____          Date    │ By Ship │  │
│                                     ────────┤Special Delivery│
│                                             │To Be Collected │
│                                             └────────────────┘
```

Figure 8.9b Delivery field is *computed* and menu driven.

Delivery field. This was defined to be a computed field, where computation is performed by a menu.

The user fills a form by using the arrow keys to move to previous/next field. No particular order is imposed on the way a form may be filled other than that specified by the attributes. Other function keys may be used to cancel a field/all fields, exit from the form, quit the form, get help from EPROS, etc. The system performs many checks on user actions to ensure correctness. One such check, for example, concerns the type of data. An example is shown in Figure 8.10a where the user attempts to assign a non-integer value to the Quantity field. In this case, the error frame will last for a short while on the screen and will disappears automatically. The field will be then cleared to allow the user to re-enter the data. Other checks ensure that the facts specified by field attributes remain integral. An example of this is shown in Figure 8.10b where the user attempts to fill the Price field before the Code field.

Once a form is filled the user may complete the task by pressing the EXIT key. The system will then check all the fields to ensure that everything is in order (for example that all non-optional fields have been filled). If not, it will give appropriate messages to guide the user in completing the form.

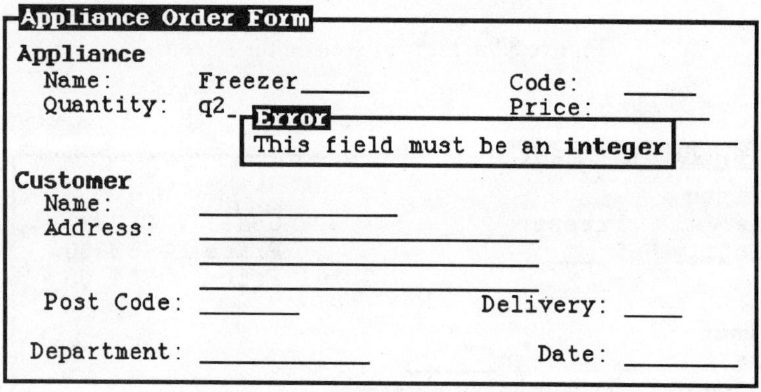

Figure 8.10a Example of a type error.

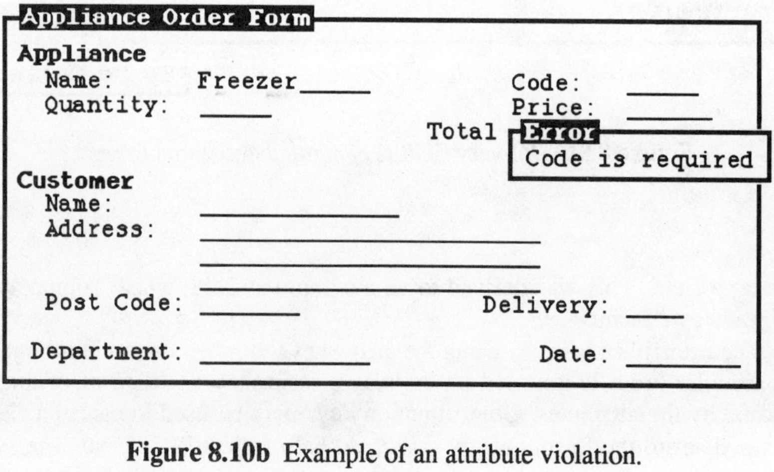

Figure 8.10b Example of an attribute violation.

8.4   Discussion

The ability to separate a dialogue from the usual processing in a program is an important one. For one thing, the dialogue part stands out, explicitly indicating where and how it fits with the rest of the system. As a result, it simplifies difficult tasks such as changing the user interface to a system and introducing multiple interfaces to the same system. Also, it encourages the developer to think of the user interface as an entity separate from the rest of the system.

The dialogue specification and development notation described in this chapter enables us to achieve such a separation. As we saw, the modularization concept is a direct extension of the familiar notion of procedural abstraction and supports hierarchical development in a similar way.

Our notation is strongly based on the STD concept and regards each separate dialogue as consisting of individual states connected through transitions which are invoked by predicates over user input and system states. Obviously, such a framework can also be represented by the implementation notation, where each state transition is realized by a `goto` statement. By restricting ourselves to a specific and tighter notation, however, we have gained the advantage of imposing a discipline which directly reflects the STD concept. The indication that a state is simple, complex, or an interaction point, for example, has on its own, enhanced the readability of dialogue specifications and has increased the amount of information that can be conveyed by a dialogue description.

We also showed how other self-contained abstractions can be exceptionally useful in dialogue development, and how they can lead to the specification and direct execution of certain interactions, rather than their time consuming implementation. A question that arises at this point is how and what other abstractions may be useful in dialogue design. This is a difficult question and can be properly answered only in the light of extensive experience. A useful criterion that we have used in this respect, and which has proved effective, is that concepts which are used repeatedly and which can be generalized should be abstracted. The provision of menus and forms, for example, reflects the use of this criterion. However, following this line of abstraction is not easy unless we have a higher order abstraction facility which allows us to *design* such abstractions with considerable ease and without disturbing the base language. This brings us to the concept of clusters and meta abstraction which is the topic of the next chapter.

8.5   Summary

A major feature of the EPROS system, which does not occur in many other prototyping systems, is its facilities for the human-computer interface. This chapter has described these facilities in some depth and shown how concepts such as forms and dialogues can be simply implemented. A number of examples in the use of these facilities were also described. It is worth stressing at this stage that the decision about which aspect of a system to prototype first: the functionality or the human–computer interface, is completely up to the staff carrying out the prototyping. EPROS allows any order.

Chapter 9
Clusters and Meta Abstraction

Two important techniques of abstraction, that is, **data abstraction** and **procedural abstraction** have already been discussed. Data abstraction was extensively covered in our discussion on abstract data types. Procedural abstraction was described in the context of FUNCTION modules. This chapter returns to the topic of procedural abstraction to introduce a new and novel abstraction technique called **cluster**. Clusters may be regarded as a generalization of current techniques for procedural abstraction and are particularly useful in situations where procedures and functions are inadequate, and unable to capture the required level of abstraction.

9.1 The need for clusters

Clusters, in fact, have already been used in this book. The menu and switch statements described in Chapter 8 are two good examples; these are predefined clusters in EPROL. To justify the need for clusters, we will go back to the problem of specifying menus and consider the difficulties that we may encounter when we attempt to realize menus using FUNCTIONs.

As stated in Chapter 8, a menu specification consists of the following.

- A menu title.
- A set of option names.
- A set of constraints, each associated with an option.
- A set of actions, one per option.

The first problem we encounter is that the number of data items is by nature variable. As a result, the data has to be passed to a function using composite data structures. Lists seem to be a good choice. Consider the following function outline.

```
FUNCTION menu(title: Str, options: Option-list): Choice;
DOM Option :: op_name: Str, cons: Bool;
    Choice = Nat;
BEGIN
/* draw the menu.
print the title.
print the options:
    if an option is active print it in bold
    otherwise print it in normal mode.
loop forever:
    cases pressed-key {
        up-arrow:   move to previous option.
        down-arrow: move to next option.
        return-key: return the option number.
    }
*/
END menu
```

Every object in the domain Option consists of an option name and its constraint. The function returns a unique id in the domain Choice which identifies the selected option. A sample call to this function is shown below.

```
cases menu ("TEST", <mk-Option("option1",pred1),
                     mk-Option("option2",pred2),
                     :
                     mk-Option("optionk",predk)>) {
    1: action1;
    2: action2;
    :
    k: actionk;
};
```

Although this approach works it has two drawbacks:

- The association of options and actions is controlled *outside* the menu function. Each call requires an additional **cases** statement to manage this. As a result, each call is longer and more complicated than it should be. Furthermore, this increases the possibility of introducing some inconsistency between options and actions. For example, suppose that during maintenance a new option is inserted in the middle of the option list. This will require a consistent re-numbering of the **cases** branches and is potentially error prone.

- The function will not allow the user to select more than one option from a menu. For example, the user cannot select option 2 then option 6 and so on. To do so, one will have to call the function repeatedly. This is unreasonable since it will display the menu each time the function is called whereas one display would be sufficient. Note that repeated calls cannot be avoided since the constraints are first evaluated and then passed as Booleans. Because the active set may change during execution, passing the constraints after each action execution is essential.

Both these problems can be avoided by passing the constraints and actions symbolically (i.e., in an unevaluated form), and managing them *inside* the menu module itself. However, function parameters are not powerful enough to support this.

9.2   The cluster module

The cluster module has been especially designed to avoid the kind of problems mentioned in the previous section. The general structure of a cluster module is shown in Figure 9.1.

```
CLUSTER  clus_id {...cluster-scheme...};
DOM    ...private domain definitions...
VAR    ...private variable definitions...
          :
        local definitions
          :
BEGIN
        :
      statements
        :
END   clus_id
```

Figure 9.1 The general structure of a CLUSTER module.

A cluster definition consists of three distinct parts: cluster scheme, local definitions, and cluster body. A cluster scheme is a syntactic description embedded with semantic descriptions such as type of objects, and effectively defines the syntactic domain of a cluster. It is composed of syntax operators and objects with predefined syntax and semantics.

The domain, variable and local definitions parts are identical to those of functions. Cluster modules may be nested in exactly the same way as other modules such as functions and dialogues. A cluster body is also very similar to that of a function; it consists of a sequence of statements.

A cluster scheme is defined using a meta notation which allows the definition of syntactic rules to describe the way in which objects may be grouped, ordered and related to each other. This notation is described below.

9.2.1   The meta notation

The meta notation is very similar to the Backus-Naur Form (BNF) notation [Naur 1963] used for specifying the syntax of programming languages. The notation is based on a number of meta characters.

The characters { and } are used to specify repetition. Objects appearing between {} may be repeated a number of times. The characters [and] specify optional objects. Any object (or group of objects) appearing between [ ] is considered to be optional. The characters (and) are used for grouping and to override the precedence of other meta characters. A vertical bar | specifies choice from a group of objects. Characters * and + are used in association with {} to specify zero or more, and one or more appearances, respectively. Finally, single quotes ' ' are used to specify literals. Literals are arbitrary sequences of characters.

For example,

```
{object}*n
```

specifies that object may appear zero or more times and that the number of appearances will be recorded in variable n. Similarly,

```
[object]n
```

specifies that object may or may not be present; n will be one if it is present and zero if not. An example of using the choice character | is

```
(object1 | object2 | object3)n
```

where one of object1, object2 or object3 must be present; n will be 1, 2 or 3 indicating which one is present. Variable n, used in the above examples, is called an **indicator**; it records a specific instance of a meta expression.

A cluster scheme is a meta expression and is composed of meta characters and

`{object}k`	object must appear k times exactly
`{object}*n`	object may appear zero or more times
`{object}+n`	object may appear one or more times
`[object]n`	object is optional
`(object)`	object itself, useful for grouping
`(object1 | object2 | object3)n`	one of object1, object2 or object3
`'charseq'`	a literal
`Exprn`	expression
`Const`	constant
`Statm`	statement
`Ident`	identifier

Figure 9.2 Summary of the meta notation.

four predefined object classes. The object classes are constants, expressions, statements and identifiers, represented by the keywords `Const`, `Exprn`, `Statm` and `Ident`, respectively. The exact syntax and semantics of these is that established by EPROL itself. A short informal description of each is given below.

- `Exprn`   a composition of variables, constants, operators, functions, etc., which when evaluated produces a value. These usually do not cause any side-effects.
- `Const`   an `Exprn` which can be, and is, evaluated at compile time.
- `Statm`   computation rules which achieve their ends through useful side-effects.
- `Ident`   a unique sequence of alphanumeric characters. Examples are variable and function names.

To avoid confusion, we should stress that literals and identifiers are totally different things. Literals have very simple semantics – they map to themselves – whereas identifiers represent objects with more elaborate meaning (e.g., a variable name). The meta notation is summarized in Figure 9.2.

Comparing the four object classes just described to parameters in a function, we observe a few differences: unlike parameters, objects are generalized, syntax directed, and may be symbolic (as opposed to a value). For this reason, we shall use the term *object* to refer to them hereafter. Similarly the terms **actual object** and **formal object** will be used in the place of actual and formal parameter.

9.2.2   Cluster schemes

In a cluster scheme, an object is specified by a unique name followed by an object class followed by a type specification (if required). For example,

> x: **Exprn:** *Real*

specifies x to be an object in the object class Exprn having the type Real. All objects require a type specification except Statm for which the type is always void, e.g.,

> s: **Statm**

specifies s to be in the object class Statm. The object class Ident can have the most general type specification. For example,

> id: **Ident:** *Nat* → *Nat-list*

specifies id to be in the object class Ident and having a function type clause which maps natural numbers to lists of natural numbers.

The meta notation provides a powerful means of grouping objects together with considerable ease. The following examples illustrate its use.

> 'if' cond: **Exprn:***Bool* 'then' st1: **Statm**
>   ['else' st2: **Statm**]n ';'

> 'begin' {st: **Statm** ';'}+n 'end'

The first example specifies an if-then-else statement where the else part is optional. The second example specifies a Pascal-like begin...end compound statement. In the second example, the object st occurs within {} and automatically becomes a list of statements. The length of this list is indicated by the value of the indicator n. So, for example, in

```
begin
    i := i+1;
    k := k-1;
    f(i,k);
end;
```

st becomes a list of three statements, i.e.:

> st = <i := i+1, k := k-1, f(i,k)>

Individual statements may be accessed by indexing the list, i.e., st[1], st[2] and st[3]. In general, every level of nesting by {} makes the formal objects within the nesting a list of whatever they are. So in

> {...{...{... ex: **Exprn:***Int* ...}*k ...}+m ...}+n

the formal object st is a list of lists of lists of integer expressions, i.e.:

```
ex: Int-list-list-list
```

The same rule equally applies to indicators. So, for example, n, m and k are of types:

```
n: Int
m: Int-list
k: Int-list-list
```

Such types are automatically set up by the EPROL compiler. Note that [ ] does not produce any nesting effects. For example, in

```
[...{... ex: Exprn:Int ...}+k ... es: Statm ...]*m
```

the types are:

```
m:  Int
es: void
k:  Int
ex: Int-list
```

9.3   A cluster definition

To illustrate the use of clusters we shall define a variant of the menu statement of EPROL as a cluster. This definition is useful in the sense that it shows how various parts of a cluster relate to each other. In particular, it shows how formal objects and indicators are manipulated. The complete definition is given below.

```
%library "scr"
%library "str"

CLUSTER menu { 'title' title: Const:Str
               { 'option' optn: Const:Str
                 [',' 'constraint' cons: Exprn:Bool]m
                 '→' action: Statm ';'
               }+n
             };
VAR  active:  array[n] Bool;
     margin:  array[n] Nat0;
     max_len: Nat0 := 0;
     cur_opn: Nat0 := 1;
```

```
    opn_len: Nat0;

    FUNCTION update_active_set ();
    VAR  actv: Bool;

    BEGIN
        for i in {1:n} do {
            if (active[i] ≠ (actv := m[i]=0 ∨ cons[i])) then {
                active[i] := actv;
                w_move (i, margin[i]);
                w_put ("%s%s",if actv then "^B" else
                            "^N", optn[i]);
            };
        };
    END update_active_set

BEGIN
    for i in {1:n} do {
        opn_len := st_len (optn[i]);
        if (opn_len > max_len) then
            max_len := opn_len;
    };
    w_open (n, max_len, title);
    for i in {1:n} do {
        margin[i] := (max_len - st_len (optn[i])) / 2 + 1;
        active[i] := m[i]=0 ∨ cons[i];
        w_move (i, margin[i]);
        w_put ("%s%s", if active[i] then "^B" else
                            "^N", optn[i]);
    };
    while TRUE do {
        w_move (cur_opn, margin[cur_opn]);
        w_put ("%s%s", if active[cur_opn] then "^M"
                    else "^R", optn[cur_opn]);
        w_move (cur_opn, 1);
        cases keybd () {
            'F1' → { w_move (cur_opn, margin[cur_opn]);
                    w_put ("%s%s", if active[cur_opn] then "^B"
                                else "^N", optn[cur_opn]);
                    cur_opn := if cur_opn = n then 1 else
                                        cur_opn+1;
                };
            'F2' → { w_move (cur_opn, margin[cur_opn]);
                    w_put ("%s%s", if active[cur_opn] then "^B"
                                else "^N", optn[cur_opn]);
```

```
                    cur_opn := if cur_opn = 1 then n else
                                                 cur_opn-1;
                };
        'F3' → if active[cur_opn] then {
                    action[cur_opn];
                    update_active_set ();
                }
                else bell ();
        'F4' → done;
        'F5' → w_text (5, 30, "^RMenu-help^N",
                                \^BF1^N - go to next option
                                ^BF2^N - go to previous option
                                ^BF3^N - select this option
                                ^BF4^N - quit this menu
                                ^BF5^N - this help\ );
        TRUE → bell ();
      };
   };
   on_exit do
          w_close (1);
END menu
```

The definition makes use of two standard libraries called scr, for screen management, and str, for string manipulation (see Appendix A). The cluster scheme is the part appearing between curly brackets just after the cluster id; title, option, ,, constraint, → and ; are all literals. The cluster scheme contains four named objects: title, optn, cons and action. The first object, title, is a string constant. The second object is a list of string constants since it occurs inside a repetition. The third object is a list of Boolean expressions, and the fourth object is a list of statements. The definition also contains two indicators: n is an integer and records the number of options, m is an integer list indicating which options have constraints.

The local variable definition part defines two dynamic arrays called active and margin of types Boolean and positive integer, respectively. Note how the indicator n is used to specify the dimension of these arrays. Array active indicates which option is active at any time. Array margin records a left margin for each option so that it will be centred. The local function update_active_set updates the active set of the menu after each action execution.

The first loop in the cluster body finds the maximum length of options, and records it in max_len. A window is then opened which is n lines long and max_len characters wide, having the title title. The next loop prints the options in this window, centering each option on a line and printing active options in bold.

The last loop executes user commands. Each time round the loop, the current option is highlighted on the screen; it is printed in mixed mode if active and in reverse video if inactive. A cases statement is used to decide which key is pressed by the user: F1 moves to the next option, F2 moves to the previous option, F3 selects an option, F4 exits from the loop, and F5 produces a help frame. Any other key is rejected by ringing the margin bell. Also note that F1 and F2 produce a wrap-around effect when the user is at the last or the first option, respectively.

Note that every reference to an Exprn or Statm object causes evaluation of that object at run time. For example, cons[i] evaluates and returns the value of the ith constraint. Const objects, on the other hand, are evaluated at compile time. It follows, therefore, that Const objects can be arbitrary expressions which do not refer to any free variables. For example, title is a Const object and in an actual call it may be

> st_conc ("Menu ", "2.5")

where st_conc is a string concatenation function. This expression is evaluated at compile time and is replaced by the constant "Menu 2.5".

An example of a call to the menu cluster is shown below. It has the same effect as the one corresponding to Figure 8.6 in Chapter 8. The only difference is that this call contains two more literals (i.e., title and option) and that is because of the way we have defined our cluster.

```
menu {
    title  "^RDB-operation^N"
    option "Insert record", constraint size < MAX_SIZE →
        ins_rec();
    option "Change record", constraint size > 0          →
        chg_rec();
    option "Delete record", constraint size > 0          →
        del_rec();
    option "Help" → menu {
                        title  "^RHelp^N"
                        option "Insert" →  ...;
                        option "Change" →  ...;
                        option "Delete" →  ...;
                        option "Back to last menu" → exit;
                        };
};
```

9.4   Termination mechanisms

There are four ways in which a cluster may be terminated. These are:

- By a static return statement in the cluster body.
- By a dynamic return statement in a cluster call.
- By a dynamic exit statement in a cluster call.

- By flow of control reaching the end of the cluster body.

Often before returning from a cluster we would like to ensure that certain tasks are properly terminated. For example, in our menu cluster, we must ensure that the menu window is closed before exiting from the cluster. One way to achieve this is to require each return statement to be preceded by a w_close(1) statement. However, such a solution is very unwise since it exposes a major design decision to the user and places considerable burden upon him. An alternative approach, offered by the cluster mechanism, is to use an on_exit do statement. This specifies a statement which is always executed before leaving the cluster.

To illustrate the features of the termination mechanism consider the following example. It is a partially defined function which contains a nested call to the menu cluster.

```
FUNCTION foo(): Int;
BEGIN
    :
    menu {
        title   "^RDB-operation^N"
        :
        option "Help" → menu {
                            title "^RHelp^N"
                            option "Insert" →  ...;
                            option "Change" →  ...;
                            option "Delete" →  ...;
                            option "Quit this menu"      → exit;
                            option "Quit previous menu" → return(0);
                        };
    };
    :
END foo
```

The exit statement in the above example terminates the inner call. This causes the on_exit do statement for the inner menu call to be executed. Hence the window of this menu will be closed and control will be transferred to the outer menu. This is an example of a dynamic exit statement. The return statement above is static with respect to the function foo, and dynamic with respect to both menu calls. When executed it first causes the on_exit do statement of the inner menu to be executed and then the on_exit do statement of the outer menu. Therefore, both menu windows will be closed successively. The function foo will be then terminated and the value 0 will be returned as the result of the function.

As a general rule, therefore, it can be stated that:

- A dynamic exit terminates the most recently invoked cluster (which is still active).

- A dynamic `return` terminates all clusters in a nested call (which are still active) until a module body is reached.

9.5   Applications of clusters

The most important use of clusters is for modular software design. Two advantages may be gained here. Firstly, the notational power of clusters simplifies the task of properly decomposing a system into modules according to the important criterion laid down by Parnas [1972, 1979]. This criterion states that when designing a system all the decisions about representation should be hidden from the programmer. This is particularly important for clusters: they have a far greater potential for information hiding than functions. For example, in the function version of menu we had to expose a major design decision to the user and require him to manage the association of options and actions outside the function. This decision was properly hidden by the cluster version which managed the association inside the cluster.

Secondly, clusters facilitate the construction of truly reusable software modules. The primary reason for this is that, unlike functions which are based on rigid interfaces, clusters allow the programmer to program the interface. In this way one can cater for a variety of call requirements without exposing any internal details of a module.

A further use of clusters is for pseudo language extension. Using this approach, a number of constructs may be added to the base language to support and simplify the task of implementing specific applications. An interesting area here is user interface design, where clusters may be used for designing dialogue facilities as abstractions. One general abstraction of this kind is what we may call a **dialogue box** and is described below.

9.5.1   Dialogue boxes

In window-oriented user interfaces usually all dialogue takes place within windows. Earlier, we saw two styles of such windows (i.e., menus and forms). A further style is what might be called a dialogue box. A dialogue box has some similarity to a menu or a form in the sense that it embodies a dialogue with a predefined protocol. Unlike menus and forms, however, the protocol is controlled by the programmer and may vary considerably from one dialogue box to another.

We illustrate the concept by an example. The following is a dialogue box definition taken from a library system which will be described in Chapter 10. The corresponding dialogue box frame is shown in Figure 9.3. The dialogue box defines a number of fields and commands for assistants adminstering loans in a library system.

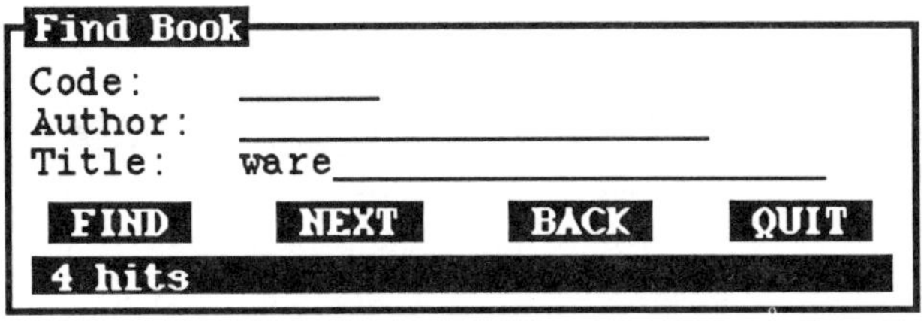

Figure 9.3 A dialogue box for finding books.

Each field consists of a field name, a field variable, the length of the field, and a value which denotes an empty field. In the fields part, the symbol → specifies the transfer of control to commands. Each command consists of a command name and a corresponding action. In the commands part, the symbol → specifies the association of an action with a command, and also the transfer of control to fields.

```
dial_box {
    "^M Find Book ^N"
    field " Code: ",    code: 6,  empty 0 → commands;
    field " Author: ",  auth: 20, empty "";
    field " Title: ",   title: 25, empty "";
    command " FIND " → { books := find_books(code,auth,title);
                         count := 1;
                         cases len books {
                             0     → message(6,WARN,...);
                             1     → fm_view(hd books,"");
                             TRUE  → message(6,NOTE,...);
                         };
                       };
    command " NEXT " → { if books = <> then
                             message(6,WARN,...)
                         else {
                             fm_view(hd books,...),
                             count := count+1;
                             books := tl books;
                             message(6,NOTE,...);
                         };
                       };
    command " BACK " → message(6,NOTE,"") → fields;
    command " QUIT " → exit;
};
```

The effect of the above dialogue box is that it first allows the user to supply a book code. If the user does so control will be transferred to the commands. The user can then select a command and execute it. If no book code is given, the user will be asked for an author name and a book title. If either of these, or both, is given then control will be transferred to the commands, otherwise the whole process will be repeated, i.e. the user will be asked for a book code, etc. When in the command section, the user can FIND books, look at the NEXT book if more than one book is found, go BACK to the fields part, or QUIT the dialogue box. The number of fields and commands is only limited by the physical size of the screen.

As illustrated in Chapter 8, complex states allow the abstraction of an entire STD. Clusters allow the abstraction of STDs along other dimensions; a recurring pattern in STDs can be abstracted and supported by a cluster-defined notation. For example, the dialogue box above corresponds to a specific pattern in the STDs of a library system (see Appendix A).

9.6 Discussion

A higher order abstraction technique based on user-defined syntax rules which, in contrast to normal abstraction techniques, allows one to treat non-elementary components of a language such as statements and expressions as objects, can be a highly useful tool in software development. It allows one to manipulate the very things a language is composed of, and to extend the base language in directions which cannot, in general, be predicted in advance.

An additional level of abstraction of this kind has two advantages: it allows the formulation and encapsulation of concepts which have been developed by others, but which cannot be conveniently captured by conventional means, and important abstractions can be developed and integrated into the base language, thereby extending its capabilities towards the needs of its users. One can also envisage the use of this form of abstraction for deriving, from the base language, languages which are geared towards specialized applications. The potential of all this for prototyping is obviously tremendous.

Some of the meta abstraction techniques described in this chapter are also available in certain programming languages. Clusters, for example, share with LISP the idea of direct manipulation of expressions in an unevaluated form. The concept of a programmable syntax-driven module interface, however, is unique to clusters and is not supported by any other language.

9.7 Summary

This chapter has described one of the major features of EPROL: the cluster. This enables a large degree of succinctness to be achieved, at the same time as enabling reusable software to be developed. The need for clusters was established and the cluster mechanism described. The chapter concluded with some examples of clusters in action.

Chapter 10
Case Study 2
An Automated Library System

This chapter further illustrates the EPROS approach to software development by describing a second case study. This is based on a computerized system to automate the daily functions of a conventional library. The system to be discussed corresponds to a real world problem of considerable size. It puts into practice the techniques described in earlier chapters in the context of a relatively realistic project, and provides further examples of specifications.

10.1 The problem

The requirements for the system were derived from the procedures for an existing manual library. After an initial study a simplified set of requirements were derived. The major simplifications of the requirements were:

• The system will only deal with books and no other form of publication.

- A keyboard will be used as the data entry device instead of a light pen.
- The system will be single user to avoid concurrency problems.
- Apart from the usual reports, the system will not generate any statistical data on the activities of the library.
- A year will be assumed to consist of 12 months, each 30 days long.

The actual requirements will not be presented in full here; they are covered by a formal specification of the system in the next section. The following is a short informal overview of the requirements.

- The library must provide functions for dealing with reader registration/deregistration and issuing, discharging, reserving, recalling and renewing of books.
- Each reader must register with the library. Each registered reader is allocated an id number.
- For each registered reader the system must record: reader's particulars (e.g., name), joining date, expected leaving date and the books he has on loan.
- Each book is allocated a code number for the purpose of identification.
- For each book the system must record the author, title, volume number, etc.
- A reader may borrow up to 40 books.
- The loan period for a book is 14 days. After this period the reader must renew the book or return it to the library.
- If a reader does not return or renew a book after 14 days it will be recalled by the library.
- If a recalled book is not returned after 30 days it will be recalled again.
- A book may be recalled up to 4 times.
- If a reader does not return a book after 200 days it will be assumed lost.
- A reader whose entire loan is assumed lost is deregistered immediately and may not borrow again from the library.
- A reader is deregistered when he leaves, provided all loans have been returned to the library.
- A reader who has left but has not returned his loan will remain registered until he does so, or until the entire loan is assumed lost. In the meantime the reader will not be allowed to borrow any more books.
- A book already on loan to a reader may be reserved by any other reader, provided the reserving reader is within the loan limit.
- There is no limit on the number of readers who may reserve the same book.
- There is no limit on the number of books a reader may reserve.
- When a reserved book becomes available it will be offered to the first person

in the reservation queue. The reader is given 14 days to collect the book, otherwise it will be offered to the next reader in the queue.

- The library records should be updated on a daily basis.
- The system should produce reports of new readers, new books, deregistered readers, lost books, released books, additions to the stock, etc.

10.2   Formal specification of the system

We represent the library by a class of states, called Lib, as defined below.

```
Lib :: rds:  Id    → Reader,  /* registered readers */
       stk:  Code  → Book,    /* library stock */
       loan: Code  → Loan,    /* current loans */
       top:  Top;             /* top indicators */
```

The component rds maps each unique reader identifier to the information held about the reader; stk maps a unique book code to the information held about the book; loan maps the code for each book on loan to the information held about the loan; and top holds other information such as the last code and id. number allocated and the current date.

Each reader is recorded by an object in

```
Reader :: name: Name,         /* reader's name */
          join: Date,         /* joining date */
          leav: Date,         /* leaving date */
          loan: Code-set;     /* books borrowed */
```

where join and leav are the reader's joining and leaving dates, and loan is the set of codes of books the reader has on loan. Each book is recorded by an object in Book:

```
Book :: auth: Author,         /* author's name */
        titl: Title,          /* book title */
        vol:  Volume;         /* book volume no. */
```

A loan is recorded by an object in

```
Loan :: date: Date,           /*date of loan/renew/discharge */
        rd:   [Id],           /* reader */
        res:  Reserve-list,   /* reservation list */
        rec:  Recall;         /* no. of recalls */
```

where date is the date of loan, renewal or discharge, rd is the id of the reader who has borrowed the book (this is NIL if he has returned it), res is the list of readers who have reserved the book, and rec is the the number of times the book has been recalled by the library.

A reservation is recorded by an object in

```
Reserve :: date: Date,        /* date of reservation */
           rd:   Id,          /* reader */
           till: [Date];      /* reserved until */
```

where date is the date of reservation, rd is the reader who has reserved the book, and till is the date by which the book must be borrowed when it is released (this is NIL when not applicable).

The domain Top is specified by the following abstract syntax rule.

```
Top :: code: Code,        /* last book code */
       id:   Id,          /* last reader id. */
       date: Date;        /* current date */
```

where code and id are the last allocated book code and reader id, and date is the current date. Finally, Report is the domain of reports produced by the system:

```
Report :: lvs: Id-set,       /* leavers - with no loan */
          dis: Id-set,       /* dishonoured readers */
          rcs: Code-set,     /* recalled books */
          rss: Code-set,     /* reserved books available */
          lst: Code-set,     /* lost books */
          rsf: Code → Reserve-list;
                             /* reserve failures due to loss */
```

We impose the following data type invariant upon the Lib.

```
inv-Lib((rds,stk,loan,top)) ≙
    dom loan ⊆ dom stk ∧
    (∀ id ∈ dom rds:
     let rd = rds(id) in
      (let ln = rd.loan in
       (∀ cd ∈ ln: cd ∈ dom loan ∧ loan(cd).rd = id) ∧
       (let el = {cd: cd ∈ ln ∧ top.date - loan(cd).date > 200}
            in (rd.leav > top.date ∨
                (ln ≠ {} ∧ (∀ cd ∈ ln: loan(cd).rec > 0))) ∧
      card ln ≤ 40 ∧ (card ln = 0 ∨ card ln > card el)))) ∧
      (∀ cd ∈ dom loan:
       let (-,rd,rs,rc) = loan(cd) in
          (rd ≠ NIL ∨ rs ≠ <> ∨ rc > 0) ∧
```

```
(rd = NIL ∧ rc = 0 ∧ rs ≠ <> ⇒
((hd rs).till ≠ NIL ∧ (hd rs).till > top.date)) ∧
rc ≤ 4 ∧
(rd = NIL ∨ (∃! rd ∈ rng rds: cd ∈ rd.loan) ∧
            cd ∈ rds(rd).loan) ∧
(let rss = elems rs in
    (∀ rz ∈ rss: rz.rd ≠ rd ∧
      (rz.till = NIL ∨ top.date > rz.till))));
```

The data type invariant states that:

- Every book on loan must have been in the stock.
- Every book borrowed by a reader must have been recorded as a loan, which indicates the correct reader of the book.
- Consider the set of books borrowed by a reader; also consider a subset of such books which have been completely expired and considered lost, we must have: either the reader has not yet left or has left and has some books on loan all of which have been recalled; and that the number of books borrowed by a reader is within the 40 books limit and either he has no books on loan at all or at least one of these books is still not considered lost.
- Every book recorded to be on loan is either still on loan, or reserved by one or more readers, or recalled and is being checked.
- If a borrowed book is returned and currently not recalled but reserved by some reader(s), then the first reservation in the queue must still be valid.
- A borrowed book may be recalled up to four times.
- A book on the loan record either has currently no reader or is borrowed by exactly one reader for whom such a record is made.
- A borrowed book cannot be reserved by its current reader and, for every reader who has reserved the book, he is either not still allowed to have the book or is given a short period to do so which is still not expired.

The following operation initializes the library. The library will initially have no readers, books, etc.; the starting day will be 0.

```
INIT: → ;
    post(-,lib') ≙ lib' = mk-Lib([],[],[],mk-Top(0,0,0));
END INIT
```

NEW_READ registers a new reader. A new reader is given a unique identifier (id) upon registration for the purpose of future reference. This identifier is returned by this operation.

```
NEW_READ: Name, Days → Id;
    post((rds,stk,loan,top),name,days,lib',id) ≙ lib' =
        mk-Lib(rds + [top.id+1 ↦ mkReader(name,top.date,
        top.date+days,{})],stk,loan,mkTop(top.code,top.id+1
        ,top.date)) ∧ id = top.id+1;
END NEW_READ
```

REM_READ deregisters a reader. The reader must have already joined the library and
have no books on loan. Upon deregistration any reservations made by the reader
are cancelled. Also, each book returned by the reader is removed from the loan
records, provided it is not reserved by another reader and the recall process (if any)
has terminated. This operation returns the set of books released because of a
deregistration.

```
REM_READ: Id → Code-set;
    exep((rds,-,loan,-),id) ≙
        id ∉ dom rds         → "No such reader",
        rds(id).loan ≠ {}  → "Has still books on loan";
    post((rds,stk,loan,top),id,lib',cs) ≙
        (let ln = [cd ↦ l: cd ∈ dom loan ∧
                  (let (dt,rd,rs,rc) = loan(cd) in
                  l = mk-Loan(dt,rd,del_id(rs,id),rc))] in
                        cs = {cd: cd ∈ dom ln ∧
                  (let (-,rd,rs,rc) = ln(cd) in
                  rd = NIL ∧ rs = <> ∧ rc = 0)} ∧
                  lib' = mk-Lib(rds ◁ {id},stk,ln ◁ cs,top));
END REM_READ
```

REM_READ uses an auxiliary function called del_id. This is defined as follows.

```
del_id: Reserve-list, Id → Reserve-list;
del_id(rs,id) ≙ mac {
    rs = <>              → <>,
    (hd rs).rd = id   → tl rs,
    TRUE                → <hd rs> ⁀ del_id(tl rs,id),
};
```

NEW_BOOK adds a new book to the stock. Each new book is given a unique code for
future reference, which is returned by the operation.

```
NEW_BOOK: Author, Title, Volume → Code;
    post((rds,stk,loan,top),auth,titl,vol,lib',code) ≙
        lib' = mk-Lib(rds,
                    stk + [top.code+1 ↦ mk-Item(auth,titl,vol)],
                    loan,
```

```
                        mk-Top(top.code+1,top.id,top.date)) ∧
        code = top.code+1;
END NEW_BOOK
```

REM_BOOK removes a book from the stock records. The book must already be in the stock. It is deleted from the stock and loan records. This operation returns the set of reservation records for the removed book.

```
REM_BOOK: Code → Reserve-list;
    exep(lib,code) ≜ code ∉ dom lib.stk → "No such book";
    post((rds,stk,loan,top),code,lib',rsv) ≜
        rsv = loan(code).res ∧
        lib' = mk-Lib(rds,stk ◁ {code},loan ◁ {code},top);
END REM_BOOK
```

ISSUE issues a book to a reader. The reader must have already been registered with the library and the book must already be in the stock records and must not be on loan. The reader's registration must not have expired and he must be within his borrowing limit. The book is issued by recording it in the reader's loan record and also in the main loan record. If the book has been reserved by the reader then the reservation record is deleted.

```
    ISSUE: Id, Code → ;
        exep((rds,stk,loan,top),id,code) ≜
        id ∉ dom rds              → "No such reader",
        code ∉ dom stk            → "No such book",
        code ∈ dom loan ∧
        (let ln = loan(code) in
                ln.rd ≠ NIL ∨ ln.rec ≠ 0 ∨
                (ln.res ≠ <> ∧ (hd ln.res).rd ≠ id))
                                  → "Already on loan",
        rds(id).leav < top.date   → "Reader's Reg. expired",
        card {cd: cd ∈ rds(id).loan ∧ loan(cd).rd = id} > 40
                                  → "Borrow limit reached";

    post((rds,stk,loan,top),id,code,lib') ≜ lib' =
        mk-Lib(rds † [id ↦ let (nm,jn,lv,ln) = rds(id) in
                            mk-Reader(nm,jn,lv,ln ∪ {code})],
                stk,
                loan † [code ↦ mk-Loan(top.date,id,
                                    if code ∈ dom loan
                                    then tl loan(code).res
                                    else <>,0)],
                top);
        END ISSUE
```

DISCHARGE discharges a book. The book must be in the stock records and already on loan. If the book is reserved by another reader, the reader is notified of the release of the book. The book is removed from the reader's loan record, but not from the main loan records for the moment; this will be done by the operation DAILY. DISCHARGE returns the id of the reader who has reserved the book (if any).

```
DISCHARGE: Code → [Id];
    exep(lib,code) ≙
        code ∉ dom lib.stk  → "No such book",
        code ∉ dom lib.loan → "Is not on loan";

    post((rds,stk,loan,top),code,lib',id) ≙
        let (-,rd,rs,rc) = loan(code) in
        let ln = mk-Loan(top.date,NIL,
                    if rs ≠ <> ∧ rc = 0 then
                        let (dt,rd,-) = hd rs in
                        <mk-Reserve(dt,rd,top.date+14)> ⁀ tl rs
                    else rs, rc) in
                lib' = mk-Lib(rds † [loan(code).rd ↦
                            let (nm,jn,lv,ln) = rds(loan(code).rd)
                            in mk-Reader(nm,jn,lv,ln - {code})],
                        stk,loan † [code ↦ ln],top) ∧
            id = (if rs ≠ <> ∧ rc = 0 then (hd rs).rd
                    else NIL);
END DISCHARGE
```

RENEW renews a book. The book must be in the stock records and already on loan. A book can be renewed provided it is neither recalled by the library nor reserved by another reader. A book is renewed by making its loan date the current date.

```
RENEW: Code → ;
    exep((-,stk,loan,top),code) ≙
        code ∉ dom stk     → "No such book",
        code ∉ dom loan    → "Is not on loan",
        loan(code).rec ≠ 0  → "Recalled - can't renew",
        loan(code).res ≠ <> → "Reserved - can't renew";

    post((rds,stk,loan,top),code,lib') ≙ lib' =
        mk-Lib(rds,stk,loan † [code ↦ mk-Loan(top.date,
                                loan(code).rd,<>,0)],
                top);
END RENEW
```

RESERVE reserves a book for a reader. The book must be in the stock records and already on loan. A book cannot be reserved by the person who currently has it on loan. No book may be reserved more than once by the same reader. A book is reserved by adding the reader's id and the date of reservation to the end of the reservation queue.

```
RESERVE: Id, Code → ;
    exep((-,stk,loan,-),id,code) ≙
        code ∉ dom stk    → "No such book",
        code ∉ dom loan    → "Is not on loan",
        loan(code).rd = id    → "You have the book - can't
                                   reserve",
        loan(code).res ≠ <> ∧
        (∃ rs ∈ elems loan(code).res: rs.rd = id)
                                → "Already reserved for you";
    post((rds,stk,loan,top),id,code,lib') ≙
        let (dt,rd,rs,rc) = loan(code) in
            lib' = mk-Lib(rds,stk,loan †
                [code ↦ mk-Loan(dt,rd,rs ⌢
                <mk-Reserve(top.date,id,NIL)>,rc)],top);
END RESERVE
```

When a recalled book is returned to the library it is checked. Such a book must already be on loan. After the book is checked the loan record is updated to terminate the recall process.

```
CHECKED: Code → ;
    exep((-,-,loan,-),code) ≙
        code ∉ dom loan    → "Is not on loan",
        loan(code).rec = 0 → "Was not recalled";
    post((rds,stk,loan,top),code,lib') ≙
        lib' = mk-Lib(rds,stk,
                loan † [code ↦ let (dt,rd,rs,-) = loan(code) in
                                    mk-Loan(dt,rd,rs,0)],
                top);
END CHECKED
```

The following operation (DAILY) must be performed once every day. It updates the information held about the library, and is interpreted as follows. The set of readers who have left the library (i.e., registration expired) is called ex. Reservations on books on loan are updated by removing those which have expired. The set of books which are considered lost is called ls. The set of dishonoured readers (i.e., those whose entire loan is considered lost) is called dis. The set of readers whose registration is expired and have no books on loan is called lvs. The set of books to be recalled (i.e., those whose loan expiry date or recall date has been reached and those borrowed by readers whose registration is now expired) is called rcs. The set of reserved books which are returned and need notifications to be sent to the readers who have reserved them is called rss. The set of books which are considered lost and were borrowed by readers who are now dishonoured is called lst. Reservations which have failed due to loss of books is called rsf.

Leavers (lvs), dishonoured readers (dis), recalls (rcs), reservation successes (rss), lost books (lst) and reservation failures (rsf) are returned by the operation as a report. The library is updated by: removing leavers and dishonoured readers from the reader records, removing lost books from the stock records and the loan records, and reporting to the readers books which were reserved and are now released. A note is made of how many times each book has been recalled. Finally, the date is updated by simply incrementing it.

```
DAILY: → Report;
   post((rds,stk,loan,top),lib',rep) ≙
     let ex = {id: id ∈ dom rds ∧ rds(id).leav < top.date},
        lon = [cd ↦ ln: cd ∈ dom loan ∧
                  ln = (let (dt,rd,rs,rc) = loan(cd) in
                        if rd = NIL ∧ rs ≠ <> ∧ rc = 0 ∧
                           (hd rs).till ≠ NIL ∧
                           (hd rs).till < top.date
                        then mk-Loan(dt,rd,tl rs,rc)
                        else loan(cd))],
        ls  = {cd:cd ∈dom loan ∧top.date - loan(cd).date > 200} in
     let dis = {id: id ∈ dom rds ∧ rds(id).loan ≠ {} ∧
                      rds(id).loan ⊆ ls} in
     let lvs = {id: id ∈ ex ∧ rds(id).loan = {}},
        rcs = {cd: cd ∈ dom lon ∧
                  (let (dt,rd,rs,rc) = lon(cd) in
                   rd ≠ NIL & rc < 4 ∧
                   lon(cd).rec*30+14 < top.date - dt)} ∪
                (∪ {rds(id).loan: id ∈ ex} -
                {cd: cd ∈ dom lon ∧ lon(cd).rec > 0}),
        rss = {cd: cd ∈ dom lon ∧ (let (-,rd,rs,rc) = lon(cd) in
                     rd = NIL ∧ rs ≠ <> ∧
                     rc = 0 ∧ (hd rs).till = NIL)},
        lst = {cd: cd ∈ ls ∧ lon(cd).rd ∈ dis} in
     let rsf = [cd ↦ lon(cd).res: cd ∈ lst ∧ lon(cd).res ≠ <>] in
        rep = mk-Report(lvs,dis,rcs,rss,lst,rsf) ∧
        lib' = mk-Lib(rds ◁ (lvs ∪ dis),stk ◁ lst,
                  [cd ↦ ln:
                     cd ∈ (dom lon - lst) ∧
                     (let (dt,rd,rs,rc) = lon(cd) in
                      ln = mk-Loan(dt,rd,
                          if cd ∈ rss then <mk-Reserve(
                              (hd rs).date,(hd rs).rd,
                              top.date+14)> ⌢ tl rs
```

$$else \text{ rs},$$
$$if \text{ cd} \in \text{rcs } then \text{ rc+1 } else \text{ rc}))],$$
$$mk\text{-Top}(top.code, top.id, top.date+1));$$

END DAILY

10.3   Evaluation

Having specified the system, we can now execute the specification to observe its behaviour. This is shown below, where the library system is tested by adding a few readers and books to the system and then executing some of the operations.

```
>> ec -q LIB          /* compile: the system is is file
                         LIB1.e */
>> ei LIB1            /* interpret */
expr> VAR lib: Lib;;
expr> `
stat> INIT(lib);
stat> `lib;
([], [], [], (0, 0, 0))
stat> ppr(NEW_READ(lib,"Mark",0));
1
stat> ppr(NEW_READ(lib,"Tony",4));
2
stat> ppr(NEW_BOOK(lib,"S.R. Bourne","The UNIX System",0));
1
stat> ppr(NEW_BOOK(lib,"B. Kernighan","Software Tools",0));
2
stat> ppr(NEW_BOOK(lib,"P. Brown","Portability",0));
3
stat> `lib;
([1 ↦ ("Mark",0,10,{}),
   2 ↦ ("Tony",0,4,{})],
  [1 ↦ ("S.R. Bourne","The UNIX System",0),
   2 ↦ ("B. Kernighan","Software Tools",0),
   3 ↦ ("P. Brown","Portability",0)],
  [], (3, 3, 0))
stat> ISSUE(lib,2,1);
stat> ISSUE(lib,2,2);
stat> ISSUE(lib,3,1);
*** EXCEPTION in ISSUE: Already on loan
stat> `lib;
([1 ↦ ("Mark",0,10,{}),
   2 ↦ ("Tony",0,4,{1,2})],
```

```
     [1 ↦ ("S.R. Bourne","The UNIX System",0),
      2 ↦ ("B. Kernighan","Software Tools",0),
      3 ↦ ("P. Brown","Portability",0)],
     [1 ↦ (0,2,<>,0), 2 ↦ (0,2,<>,0)],
     (3,3,0))
stat> RESERVE(lib,3,1);
stat> RESERVE(lib,3,3);
*** EXCEPTION in RESERVE: Is not on loan
stat> RESERVE(lib,1,1);
stat> `lib;
([1 ↦ ("Mark",0,10,{}),
   2 ↦ ("Tony",0,4,{1,2})],
  [1 ↦ ("S.R. Bourne","The UNIX System",0),
   2 ↦ ("B. Kernighan","Software Tools",0),
   3 ↦ ("P. Brown","Portability",0)],
  [1 ↦ (0,2,<(0,3,NIL),(0,1,NIL)>,0), ↦(0,2,<>,0)],
  (3,3,0))
stat> ppr(DISCHARGE(lib,1));
3
stat> ppr(DAILY(lib));
([1 ↦ ("Mark",0,10,{}),
   2 ↦ ("Tony",0,4,{2})],
  [1 ↦ ("S.R. Bourne","The UNIX System",0),
   2 ↦ ("B. Kernighan","Software Tools",0),
   3 ↦ ("P. Brown","Portability",0)],
  [1 ↦ (0,NIL,<(0,3,14), (0,1,NIL)>,0), 2 ↦
(0,2,<>,0)],
  (3,3,1))
stat>
```

10.4 Verification

Since the specification outlined here is the top level specification of the system, verification at this stage only involves showing that the operations of the abstract data type preserve the data type invariant (i.e., that they are valid). This is demonstrated below for the first two operations.

Lemma 10.1

INIT is valid.

Proof

We must show that:

$$pre(\text{lib}) \land inv(\text{lib}) \land post(\text{lib},\text{lib}') \Rightarrow inv(\text{lib}')$$

According to *post*:

```
lib' = mk-Lib([],[],[],mk-Top(0,0,0))
```

Therefore

$$dom \text{ rds} = dom \text{ loan} = \{\}$$

which proves that

```
inv(lib') = TRUE
```
□

Lemma 10.2

NEW_READ is valid.

Proof

We must show that:

$$pre(\text{lib},\text{name},\text{days}) \land inv(\text{lib}) \land post(\text{lib},\text{name},\text{days},\text{lib}',\text{id})$$
$$\Rightarrow inv(\text{lib}')$$

We have:

$$inv((\text{rds}',\text{stk}',\text{loan}',\text{top}')) \triangleq$$

$dom \text{ loan}' \subseteq dom \text{ stk}'$	(1)
$(\forall \text{ id} \in dom \text{ rds}': \ldots.) \land$	(2)
$(\forall \text{ cd} \in dom \text{ loan}': \ldots.);$	(3)

Using *post*:

$$\text{stk}' = \text{stk} \land \text{loan}' = \text{loan}$$

Hence (1) follows from *inv*(lib). Also

$$rng \text{ rds}' = rng \text{ rds} \cup \text{mk-Reader}(\ldots,\{\})$$

So (3) holds too. It remains to show that (2) holds. Using *inv*(lib) and *post*, (2) reduces to:

```
let rd = rds(id) in
  (let ln = rd.loan in
    (∀ cd ∈ ln: cd ∈ dom loan ∧ loan(cd).rd = id) ∧
    (let el = {cd: cd ∈ln∧top.date - loan(cd).date > 200} in
      (rd.leav > top.date ∨
```

$$(\text{ln} \neq \{\} \wedge (\forall \text{ cd} \in \text{ln: loan(cd).rec} > 0))) \wedge$$
$$card \text{ ln} \leqslant 40 \wedge (card \text{ ln} = 0 \vee card \text{ ln} > card \text{ el})))$$

Using $post$, rd.loan = {}; hence ln = el = {}. Using $post$ again, top'.date+days = leav', since days $\in$ Nat. Hence rd'.leav > top'.date and it follows that:

inv(lib') = TRUE

The validity of other operations can be proved in a similar way. $\square$

10.5   Refinement of specification

The above specification should be refined a number of times before it can be realized as a concrete program. During each such refinement, design decisions are made about the way the data should be represented, and further details are introduced into the system. For example, whereas in our original specification a reader's record consists of his name, joining date, leaving date, and current loan only, in the subsequent refinements more information, such as the reader's address, job title, etc., may be included. In other words, information which were abstracted away in the original specification are gradually introduced in the refinements.

Deciding what to include in a specification and what to ignore is a difficult task. The only useful guideline one can think of is to include only those aspects

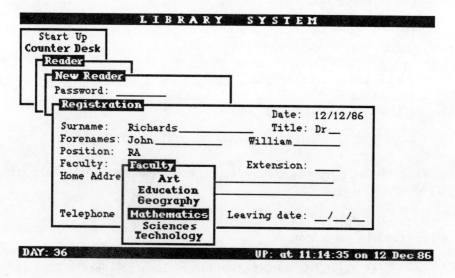

Figure 10.1 A screen view of the library system.

which are critical and of fundamental importance, that is, features whose exclusion will cause loss of meaning and generality. Refinement, in any case, is a self-regulating process and illustrates whether the original specification has been wise and suitable. When this is the case, refinement progresses smoothly and further details are included easily, thereby *expanding* the specification. However, when the original specification is ill-conceived, refinements become exceedingly difficult and error-prone. Inevitably, they force the software developer to go back to the original specification to make fundamental *changes*, or even worse, to do a complete re-formulation.

The refinement of the library system was carried out in three iterations, with a user interface being introduced during the second iteration. All the refinements were prototyped and executed using EPROS, to ensure that the design decisions are consistent. Verification, however, was only applied to the original specification. The final concrete version of the system together with a specification of the user interface may be found in Appendix B. You will find that this version is detailed enough to illustrate nearly all the EPROL facilities described in this book. Figure 10.1 shows a screen view of the user interface of the library system.

10.6   Summary

This chapter has described, in some detail, the top-level design of an automated library system. It described the steps that would normally be taken in developing a large system using VDM and the prototyping approach supported by the EPROS system. The approach regards both verification and execution as complementary activities.

References

Aaram, J. 1984. 'The BOP Prototyping Concept,' *Approaches to Prototyping*, R. Budde *et al.* (eds.), Berlin: Springer-Verlag, pp. 179-187.

Ackford R. L. 1967. 'Management Misinformation Systems,' *Management Science*, **14**(4) pp. 456-461.

Alavi, M. 1984. 'An Assessment of Prototyping Approach to Information System Development,' *Communications of the ACM*, **27**(6) pp. 556-563.

Alter, S.A. 1980. *Decision Support Systems – Current Practices and Continuing Challenges*, Reading, Mass: Addison-Wesley.

Alexander, H. 1986. *Formally-Based Tools and Techniques for Human–Computer Dialogues*, PhD Thesis, Dept. of Computing, Stirling University.

Apple 1985. *Inside Macintosh: Volumes I, II and III*, Reading, MA: Addison-Wesley.

Backus, J. 1978. 'Can Programming be Liberated from the von Neumann Style? A Functional Style and its Algebra of Programs,' *Communications of the ACM*, **21**(8) pp. 613-641.

Baldwin, R. R. 1982. 'Reportage on Spring 1982 IEEE COMPCON Conference,' *ACM SIGSOFT Software Engineering Notes*, **7**(2) pp. 13-20.

Bally, L., Brittan, J. and Wagner, K. H. 1977. 'A Prototype Approach to Information System Design and Development,' *Information and Management*, **1** pp. 21-26.

Balzer, R., Cheatham, T. E. and Green, C. 1983. 'Software Technology in the 1990s: Using a New Paradigm,' *IEEE Computer*, **16**(11) pp. 39-45

Balzer, R., Goldman, N. M. and Wile, D. S. 1982. 'Operational Specification as the Basis of Rapid Prototyping,' *ACM SIGSOFT Software Engineering Notes*, **7**(5) pp. 3-16.

Barstow, D. 1985. 'On Convergence Towards a Database of Program Transformations,' *ACM Trans. Programming Languages and Systems*, 7(1) pp. 1-9.

Basili, V. R. and Turner, D. 1975. 'Iterative Enhancement: A Practical Technique for Software Development,' *IEEE Trans. Software Engineering*, 1(4) pp. 462-471.

Bastani, F. A. 1985. 'Experience with a Feedback Version Development Methodology, *IEEE Trans. Software Engineering*,' 11(8) pp. 718-723.

Beichter, F. W., Herzog, O. and Petzsch, H. 1984. 'SLAN-4 – A Software Specification and Design Language,' *IEEE Trans. Software Engineering*, 10(2) pp. 155-162.

Belkhouche, B. 1985. 'Compilation of Specification Languages as a Basis for Rapid and Efficient Prototyping,' *Proc. 3rd Int. Workshop Software Specification and Design*, London, pp. 16-19.

Bell, T. E. Bixler, D. C. and Dyer, M. E. 1977. 'An Extendable Approach to Computer-Aided Software Requirements Engineering,' *IEEE Trans. Software Engineering*, 3(1) pp. 49-60.

Bell Laboratory 1979. *UNIX Programmer's Manual*, 7th Edition, Murray Hill, NJ: Bell Laboratory.

Benbasat I. and Wand, Y. 1984. 'A Structured Approach to Designing Human–Computer Dialogues,' *Int. Journal of Man–Machine Studies*, 21 pp. 105-126.

Berrisford T. and Wetherbe, J. 1979. 'Heuristic Development: A Redesign of Systems Design,' *MIS Quarterly*, 3(1) pp. 11-19.

Berzins V. and Gray, M. 1985. 'Analysis and Design in MSG.84: Formalizing Functional Specifications,' *IEEE Trans. Software Engineering*, 11(8) pp. 657-670.

Bird, R. S. 1984. 'The Promotion and Accumulation Strategies in Transformational Programming,' *ACM Trans. Prog. Langs. and Systems*, 6(4) pp. 487-504.

Birtwistle, G. M. *et al.* 1973. *Simula Begin*, New York: Petrocelli.

Bjorner D. and Jones C. B. (eds.) 1978. *The Vienna Development Method: The Meta-Language*, Lecture Notes in Computer Science, 61, Berlin: Springer Verlag.

Bjorner D. and Jones, C. B. 1982. *Formal Specification and Software Development*, London: Prentice-Hall.

Blesser T. and Foley, J. D. 1982. 'Towards Specifying and Evaluating the Human Factors of User–Computer Interfaces,' *Proc. Conf. Human Factors in Computer Systems*, Gaithersburg, Maryland, pp. 309-314.

Bloomfield, R. E. and Froome, P. K. D. 1986. 'The Application of Formal Methods to the Assessment of High Integrity Software,' *IEEE Trans. Software Engineering*, 12(9), pp. 988-993.

Blum, B. I. 1982. 'The Life Cycle – A Debate Over Alternate Models,' *ACM SIGSOFT Software Engineering Notes*, 7(4) pp. 18-20.

Blum, B. I. 1986. 'Iterative Development of Information Systems: A Case Study,' *Software Practice and Experience*, 16(6) pp. 503-515.

Blum, B. I. and Houghton, R. C. 1982. 'Rapid Prototyping of Information Management Systems,' *ACM SIGSOFT Software Engineering Notes*, 7(5) pp. 35-38.

Boehm, B. W. 1974. 'Some Steps Towards Formal and Automated Aids to Software Requirements Analysis and Design,' *IFIP 74*, North-Holland, pp. 192-197.

Boehm, B. W. 1981. *Software Engineering Economics*, Englewood Cliffs, NJ: Prentice-Hall.

Boehm, B. W., Gray, T. E. and Seewaldt, T. 1984. 'Prototyping Versus Specifying: A Multiproject Experiment,' *IEEE Trans. Software Engineering*, 10(3) pp. 290-303.

Boehm, B. W. and Standish, T. A. 1983. 'Software Technology in the 1990s: Using an Evolutionary Paradigm,' *IEEE Computer*, 16(1) pp. 30-37.

Bonet, R. and Kung, A. 1984. 'Structuring into Subsystems: the Experience of a Prototyping Approach,' *ACM SIGSOFT Software Engineering Notes*, 9(5) pp. 23-27.

Bos, J. 1978. 'Definition and Use of Higher-Level Graphics Input Tools,' *Computer Graphics*, 12(3) pp. 38-42.

Bos, J., Plasmeijer, M. J. and Hartel, P. H. 1983. 'Input–Output Tools: A Language Facility for Interactive and Real-Time Systems,' *IEEE Trans. Software Engineering*, 9(3) pp. 247-259.

Bosman, A. and Sol, H. G. 1981. 'Evolutionary Development of Information Systems,' *TC8 Working Conference on Evolutionary Information Systems*, Part 1.

Botting, R. J. 1985. 'On Prototyping vs. Mockups vs. Breadboards,' *ACM SIGSOFT Software Engineering Notes*, 10(1) p. 18.

Bourne, S. R. 1983. *The Unix System*, Reading, MA: Addison-Wesley.

Boyle, J. M. and Muralidharan, N. M. 1984. 'Program Reusability Through Program Transformation,' *IEEE Trans. Software Engineering*, 10(5), pp. 574-588.

Brittan, J. N. G. 1980. 'Design for a Changing Environment,' *The Computer Journal*, 23(1) pp. 13-19.

Brooks, F. 1975. *The Mythical Man-Month*, Reading, MA: Addison-Wesley.

Browne, D. P. 1986. 'The Formal Specification of Adaptive User Interfaces Using Command Language Grammar,' *Proc. CHI'86*, Boston, MA, pp. 256-260.

Brown, J. W. 1982. 'Controlling The Complexity of Menu Networks,' *Communications of the ACM*, 25(7) pp. 412-418.

Budde, R. and Sylla, K. 1984. 'From Application Domain Modelling to Target System,' *Approaches to Prototyping*, R. Budde, K. Kuhlenkamp, L. Mathiassen and H. Zullighoven (eds.), Berlin: Springer-Verlag, pp. 31-48.

Burstall, R. M., MacQueen, D. and Sanella, D. 1980. 'HOPE: an Experimental Applicative Language,' *Conf. Rec. 1980 Lisp Conf.*, Stanford University, pp. 136-143.

Burstall, R. M. and Goguen, J. A. 1981. 'An Informal Introduction to Specifications Using CLEAR,' *The Correctness problem in Computer Science*, J. Moore (ed.), New York: Academic Press.

Buxton, W. Lamb, M. R. Sherman, D. and Smith, K. C. 1983. 'Toward a Comprehensive User Interface Management System,' *Computer Graphics*, **17**(3) pp. 35-42.

Canning, R. G. 1981. 'Developing Systems by Prototyping,' *EDP Analyzer*, **19**(9) pp. 1-14.

Carey, T. 1982. 'User Differences in Interface Design,' *IEEE Computer*, **15**(3), pp. 14-20.

Casey, B. E. and Dasarathy, B. 1982. 'Modelling and Validating the Man–Machine Interface,' *Software-Practice and Experience*, **12** pp. 557-569.

Cheatham, T. E. 1984. Reusability Through Program Transformations,' *IEEE Trans. Software Engineering*, **10**(5) pp. 589-594.

Cheatham, T. E., Holloway, G. H. and Townley, J. A. 1979. 'Symbolic Evaluation and Analysis of Programs,' *IEEE Trans. Software Engineering*, **5**(4) pp. 402-417.

Cheng, T. T., Lock, E. D. and Prywes, N. S. 1984. 'Use of Very High Level Languages and Program Generation by Management Professionals,' *IEEE Trans. Software Engineering*, **10**(5) pp. 552-563.

Chi, U. I. 1985. 'Formal Specification of User Interface: A Comparison and Evaluation of Four Axiomatic Approaches,' *IEEE Trans. Software Engineering*, **11**(8) pp. 671-685.

Christensen, N. and Kreplin, K. 1984. 'Prototyping of User–Interfaces,' *Approaches to Prototyping*, R. Budde, K. Kuhlenkamp, L. Mathiassen and H. Zullighoven (eds.), Berlin: Springer-Verlag, pp. 58-67.

Clark, F., Drake, P., Kapp, M. and Wong, P. 1984. 'User Acceptance of Information Technology Through Prototyping,' *Proc. Interact 1984 Conf.*, London, pp. 274-279.

Clark, I. A. 1981. 'Software Simulation as a Tool For Usable Product Design,' *IBM System Journal*, **20**(3) pp. 272-293.

Claybrook, B. G. 1982. 'A Specification Method for Specifying Data and Procedural Abstractions,' *IEEE Trans. Software Engineering*, **8**(5) pp. 449-459.

Clocksin, W. E. and Mellish, C. S. 1984. *Programming in Prolog*, 2nd edition, Berlin: Springer-Verlag.

Cohen, D., Swartout, W. and Balzer, R. 1982. 'Using Symbolic Execution to Characterize Behaviour,' *ACM SIGSOFT Software Engineering Notes*, **7**(5) pp. 25-32.

Conway, M. E. 1963. 'Design of a Separable Transition Diagram Compiler,' *Communications of the ACM*, **6**(7) pp. 396-408.

Cook, S. 1986. 'Modelling Generic User Interface with Functional Programs,' *People and Computers: Designing for Usability* , M. D. Harrison and A. I. Monk (eds.), Cambridge: Cambridge University Press, pp. 368-385.

Cottam, I. 1984. 'Rigorous Development of a Version Control Program,' *IEEE Trans. Software Engineering*, **10**(2) pp. 143-154.

Dagwell, R. and Weber, R. 1983 'System Designers' User Models: A Comparative Study and Methodological Critique,' *Communications of the ACM*, **26**(11) pp. 987-997.

Dannenberg, R. B. and Ernst, G. W. 1982. 'Formal Program Verification Using Symbolic Execution,' *IEEE Trans. Software Engineering*, **10**(1) pp. 43-52.

Darlington, J. 1981. 'An Experimental Program Transformation and Synthesis System,' *Artificial Intelligence*, **16** pp. 1-46.

Darlington, J. 1983. 'Validation Techniques for Software Specifications,' *Microcomputers: Developments in Industry, Business and Education*, C. J. van Spronsen (ed.), Amsterdam: North-Holland, pp. 91-97.

Darlington, J. and Burstall, R. M. 1976. 'A System which Automatically Improves Programs,' *Acta Informatica*, **6** pp. 41-60.

Darlington, J., Henderson, P. and Turner, D. A. (eds.) 1982. *Functional Programming and its Applications – an Advanced Course*, Cambridge: Cambridge University Press.

Davis, A. M. 1979. 'Formal Techniques and Automatic Processing to Ensure Correctness in Requirements Specifications,' *Proc. Conf. Specification of Reliable Software*, pp. 15-35.

Davis, C. G. and Vick, C. R. 1977. 'The Software Development System,' *IEEE Trans. Software Engineering*, **3**(1) pp. 69-84.

Davis, R. 1983. 'Task Analysis and User Errors: A Methodology for Assessing Interactions,' *Int. Journal of Man–Machine Studies*, **19** pp. 561-574.

Dearnley, P. A. and Mayhew, P.J. 1981. 'Experiments in Generating System Prototypes,' *Proc. First European Workshop on Inf. Systems Teaching*, Aix-en-Provence.

Dearnley, P. A. and Mayhew, P. J. 1983. 'In Favour of System Prototypes and their Integration into the System Development Cycle,' *The Computer Journal* **26**(1) pp. 36-42.

Dearnley, P. A. and Mayhew, P. J. 1984. 'On the Use of Software Development Tools in the Construction of Data Processing System Prototypes,' *Approaches to Prototyping*, R. Budde, K. Kuhlenkamp, L. Mathiassen and H. Zullighoven (eds.), Berlin: Springer-Verlag, pp. 68-79.

Denert, E. 1977. 'Specification and Design of Dialogue Systems with State Diagrams,' *International Computing Symposium 1977*, D. Ribbens (ed.), North-Holland. pp. 417-424.

Dixon, F. J. 1985. 'Simplifying Screen Specifications – the Full Screen Manager Interface and Screen Form Generating Routines,' *The Computer Journal* **28**(2) pp. 117-127.

Dodd, W. P. 1980. 'Prototype Programs,' *IEEE Computer*, **13**(2) p. 80.

Draper, S. W. and Norman, D. A. 1985. 'Software Engineering for User Interfaces,' *IEEE Trans. Software Engineering*, **11**(3) pp. 252-258.

Drosten, K. 1984. 'Towards Executable Specifications Using Conditional Axioms,' *STACS 84*, Lecture Notes in Computer Science **166**, Berlin: Springer-Verlag, pp. 85-96.

Dyer, M. 1980. 'The Management of Software Engineering Part IV: Software Development Practices,' *IBM System Journal*, No. 4 pp. 458-459.

Earl, M. J. 1978. 'Prototype Systems for Accounting, Information and Control,' *Accounting, Organisation and Society*, **3**(2) pp. 161-170.

Edmonds, E. A. 1981. 'Adaptive Man–Computer Interfaces,' *Computing Skills and the User Interface*, M. J. Coombs and J. L. Alty, (eds.), London: Academic Press, pp. 389-426.

Edmonds, E. A. 1982. 'The Man–Computer Interface: a Note on Concepts and Design,' *Int. Journal of Man–Machine Studies*, **16** pp. 231-236.

Edmonds, E. A. and Guest, S. 1984. 'The SYNICS2 Interface Manager,' *Proc. Interact 1984 Conf.*, pp. 53-56.

Farkas, Z., Szeredi, P. and Santane-Toth, E. 1982. 'LDM – A Program Specification Support System,' *Proc. Logic Programming Workshop*, Marcei-France, pp. 123-128.

Feather, M. S. 1982a. 'Mappings for Rapid Prototyping,' *ACM SIGSOFT Software Engineering Notes*, **7**(5) pp. 17-24.

Feather, M. S. 1982b. 'Program Specification Applied to a Text Formatter,' *IEEE Trans. Software Engineering*, **8**(5) pp. 490-498.

Feyock, S. 1977. 'Transition Diagram Based CAI/HELP Systems,' *Int. Journal of Man–Machine Studies*, **9** pp. 399-413.

Floyd, C. 1984. 'A Systematic Look at Prototyping,' *Approaches to Prototyping*, R. Budde, K. Kuhlenkamp, L. Mathiassen and H. Zullighoven (eds.), Berlin: Springer-Verlag, pp. 1-18.

Foley, J. and Van Dam, A. 1982. *Fundamentals of Interactive Computer Graphics*, Reading, MA: Addison-Wesley.

Fox, J. M. 1982. *Software and its Development*, Englewood Cliffs, NJ: Prentice-Hall.

Furtado, A. L. and Maibaum, T. S. E. 1985. 'An Informal Approach to Formal (Algebraic) Specifications,' *The Computer Journal*, **28**(1) pp. 59-67.

Gaines, B. R. 1981. 'The Technology of Interaction – dialogue programming rules,' *Int. Journal of Man–Machine Studies*, **14** pp. 133-150.

Gehani, N. H. 1982a. 'A Study in Prototyping,' *ACM SIGSOFT Software Engineering Notes*, **7**(5) pp. 71-75.

Gehani, N. H. 1982b. 'The Potential of Forms in Office Automation,' *IEEE Trans. Communications*, **30**(1) pp. 120-125.

Gehani, N. H. 1983. 'High Level Form Definition in Office Information Systems,' *The Computer Journal*, **26**(1), pp. 52-59.

Gilb, T. 1981. 'Evolutionary Development,' *ACM SIGSOFT Software Engineering Notes*, **6**(2) p. 17.

Gilb, T. 1985. 'Evolutionary Delivery versus the Waterfall Model,' *ACM SIGSOFT Software Engineering Notes*, **10**(3) pp. 49-62.

Gill, H., Lindvall, R., Rosin, O., Sandewall, E., Sorensen, H. and Wigertz, O. 1982. 'Experience from Computer Supported Prototyping for Information Flow in Hospitals,' *ACM SIGSOFT Software Engineering Notes*, **7**(5) pp. 67-70.

Gittins, D. T., Winder, R. L. and Bez, H. E. 1984 'An Icon-Driven End-User Interface to UNIX,' *Int. Journal of Man–Machine Studies*, **21** pp. 451-461.

Gladden, G. R. 1982. 'Stop the Life-Cycle, I Want to Get Off,' *ACM SIGSOFT Software Engineering Notes*, **7**(2) pp. 35-39.

Goguen, J. A. 1984. 'Parameterized Programming,' *IEEE Trans. Software Engineering*, **10**(5) pp. 528-543.

Goguen, J. A. and Tardo, J. J. 1979. 'An Introduction to OBJ: A Language for Writing and Testing Formal Algebraic Program Specifications,' *Proc. Specification of Reliable Software*, pp. 170-189.

Gomaa, H. 1983. 'The Impact of Rapid Prototyping on Specifying User Requirements,' *ACM SIGSOFT Software Engineering Notes*, **8**(2) pp. 17-28.

Gomaa, H. and Scott, D. B. H. 1981. 'Prototyping as a Tool in the Specification of User Requirements,' *Proc. 5th Int. Conf. Software Engineering*, pp. 333-342.

Gordon, M. J., Milner, A. J. and Wadsworth, C. P. 1979. *Edinburgh LCF*, Lecture Notes in Computer Science, **78**, Berlin: Springer-Verlag.

Gould, J. D., Conti, J. and Hovanyecz, T. 1983. 'Composing Letters with a Simulated Listening Typewriter,' *Communications of the ACM*, **26**(4) pp. 295-308.

Gray, D. and Kilgour, A. 1985. 'Guide: A UNIX-Based Dialogue Design System,' *People and Computers: Designing the Interface*, P. Johnson and S. Cook (eds.), Cambridge: Cambridge University Press, pp. 148-160.

Green, M. 1981. 'A Methodology for the Specification of Graphics User Interface,' *Computer Graphics*, **15**(3) pp. 99-108.

Green, M. 1985. 'Design Notations and User Interface Management Systems,' *UIMS*, G. E. Pfaff (ed.), Berlin: Springer-Verlag.

Gregory, S. T. 1984. 'On Prototypes vs. Mockups,' *ACM SIGSOFT Software Engineering Notes*, **9**(5) p. 13.

Griswold, R. E., Poage, J. F. and Polonsky, I.P. 1971. *The SNOBOL4 Programming Language*, Englewood Cliffs, NJ: Prentice-Hall.

Groner, C., Hopwood, M. D., Palley, N. A. and Sibley, W. 1979. 'Requirements Analysis in Clinical Research Information Processing – A Case Study,' *IEEE Computer*, **12**(9) pp. 100-108.

Guest, S. P. 1982. 'The Use of Software Tools for Dialogue Design,' *Int. Journal of Man–Machine Studies*, **16** pp. 263-285.

Guttag, J. V. 1977. 'Abstract Data Types and the Development of Data Structures,' *Communications of the ACM*, **20**(6) pp. 396-404.

Guttag, J. V. and Horning, J. J. 1978. 'The Algebraic Specification of Abstract Data Types,' *Acta Informatica*, **10** pp. 27-52.

Hall, P. A. V. 1986. 'Reusable and Reconfigurable Software Using C,' *Software Engineering 86*, D. Barnes and P. Brown (eds.), London: Peter Peregrinus, pp. 164-174.

Hanau, P. R. and Lenorovitz, D. R. 1980. 'Prototyping and Simulation Tools for User/Computer Dialogue Design,' *Computer Graphics*, **14**(2) pp. 271-278.

Hansal, A. 1976. 'A Formal Definition of a Relational Database System,' *IBM UKSC 0080 Report*.

Hawgood, J. (ed.) 1982. *Evolutionary Information Systems*, Amsterdam: North-Holland.

Hayes, P. J., Ball, E. and Reddy, R. 1981. 'Breaking the Man–Machine Communication Barrier,' *IEEE Computer*, **14**(3) pp. 19-30.

Heitmeyer, C., Landwehr, C. and Cornwell, M. 1982. 'The Use of Quick Prototypes in the Secure Military Message Systems Project,' *ACM SIGSOFT Software Engineering Notes*, **7**(5) pp. 85-87.

Henderson, J. C. and Ingraham, R. S. 1982. 'Prototyping for DSS: A Critical Appraisal,' *Decision Support Systems*, E. A. Stohr (ed.), Amsterdam: North-Holland, pp. 79-96.

Henderson, P. 1980. *Functional Programming – Application and Implementation*, London: Prentice-Hall.

Henderson, P. 1984. 'Me-Too – A Language for Software Specification and Model Building – Preliminary Report,' *Tech. Report FPN-9*, Computing Dept., Stirling University

Henderson, P. 1986. 'Functional Programming, Formal Specification, and Rapid Prototyping,' *IEEE Trans. Software Engineering*, **12**(2) pp. 241-250.

Henderson, P. and Minkowitz, C. 1985. 'The Me-Too Method of Software Design,' *Tech. Report FPN-10*, Computing Dept., Stirling University.

Hoare, C. A. R. and Wirth, N. 1973. 'An Axiomatic Definition of the Programming Language Pascal,' *Acta Informatica*, **2** pp. 335-355.

Hooper, J. W. and Hsia, P. 1982. 'Scenario-Based Prototyping of Requirements Identification,' *ACM SIGSOFT Software Engineering Notes*, **7**(5) pp. 88-93.

Hopgood, F. R. and Duce, D. A. 1980. 'A Production Approach to Interactive Graphic Program Design,' *Methodology of Interaction*, R. A. Guedj *et al.* (eds.), Amsterdam:North-Holland, pp. 247-263.

Horowitz, E. and Munson, J. B. 1984. 'An Expansive View of Reusable Software,' *IEEE Trans. Software Engineering*, **10**(5) pp. 477-487.

Iivari, J. 1984. 'Prototyping in the Context of Information Systems Design,' *Approaches to Prototyping*, R. Budde, K. Kuhlenkamp, L. Mathiassen and H. Zullighoven (eds.), Berlin: Springer-Verlag, pp. 261-277.

Jacob, R. J. K. 1983. 'Using Formal Specifications in The Design of a Human–Computer Interface,' *Communications of the ACM*, **26**(4) pp. 259-264.

James, E. B. 1980. 'The User Interface,' *The Computer Journal*, **23**(1) pp. 25-28.

Johnson, S. C. 1975. 'Yacc: Yet Another Compiler Compiler,' *Comp. Sci. Tech. Report No. 32*, Murray Hill, NJ: Bell Labs.

Johnson, W. L. 1968. 'Automatic Generation of Efficient Lexical Processors Using Finite State Techniques,' *Communications of the ACM*, **11**(12) pp. 805-813.

Jones, C. B. 1977. 'Program Specification and Formal Development,' *International Computing Symposium 1977*, D. Ribbens (ed.), Amsterdam: North-Holland, pp. 537-553.

Jones, C. B. 1980a. *Software Development: A Rigorous Approach*, London: Prentice-Hall.

Jones, C. B. 1980b. 'The Role of Formal Specification in Software Development,' *Life Cycle Management: Infotech State of the Art Report*, **8**(7) pp. 117-133, Infotech Ltd.

Jones, C. B. 1986. *Systematic Software Development using VDM*, London: Prentice-Hall.

Kant, E. and Barstow, D. R. 1981. 'The Refinement Paradigm: The Interaction of Coding and Efficiency Knowledge in Program Synthesis,' *IEEE Trans. Software Engineering*, **7**(5) pp. 458-471.

Keen, P.G.W. 1981. 'Information Systems and Organisational Change,' *Communications of the ACM*, **24**(1), pp. 24-33.

Kemmerer, R. A. 1985. 'Testing Formal Specifications to Detect Design Errors,' *IEEE Trans. Software Engineering*, **11**(1) pp. 32-43.

Kennedy, K. and Schwartz, J. 1975. 'An Introduction to The Set Theoretical Language SETL,' *Comp. and Maths with Applications*, **1** pp. 97-119.

Kenneth, C. R. C. 1981. 'Screen Updating and Cursor Movement Optimization: A Library Package,' *Tech. Report*, Dept. of Electrical Eng. and Comp. Sci., University of California, Berkeley.

Kernighan, B. W. and Ritchie, D. M. 1978. *The C Programming Language*, Englewood Cliffs, NJ: Prentice-Hall.

Keus, H. E. 1982. 'Prototyping: A More Reasonable Approach to System Development,' *ACM SIGSOFT Software Engineering Notes*, **7**(5) pp. 94-95.

Kieras, D. and Polson, P. 1983. 'A Generalized Transition Network Representation for Interactive Systems,' *Proc. CHI 1983*, pp. 103-106.

Kowalski, R. 1979. 'Algorithm = Logic + Control,' *Communications of the ACM*, **22**(7) pp. 424-436.

Kraushaar, J. M. and Shirland, L. E. 1985. 'A Prototyping Method for Applications Development by End Users and Information Systems Specialists,' *MIS Quarterly*, **9**(2), pp. 189-197.

Kruchten, P. and Schonberg, E. 1984. 'The Ada/Ed System: A Large-scale Experiment in Software Prototyping Using SETL,' *Approaches to Prototyping*, R. Budde, K. Kuhlenkamp, L. Mathiassen and H. Zullighoven (eds.), Berlin: Springer-Verlag, pp. 398-415.

Kruesi, E. 1983. 'The Human Engineering Task Area,' *IEEE Computer*, **16**(1), pp. 86-93.

Lafuente, J. M. and Gries, D. 1978. 'Language Facilities for Programming User–Computer Dialogues,' *IBM Journal of Research and Development.* **22**(2) pp. 145-158.

Lanergan, R. G. and Grasso, C. A. 1984. 'Software Engineering with Reusable Designs and Code,' *IEEE Trans. Software Engineering,* **10**(5), pp. 498-501.

Leavenworth, B. M. and Sammet, J. E. 1974. 'Overview of Non-Procedural Languages,' *ACM SIGPLAN Notices,* **9**(2) pp. 98-103.

Lee, S. and Sluizer, S. 1985. 'On Using Executable Specifications for High-Level Prototyping,' *Proc. 3rd Int. Workshop Software Specification and Design,* London, pp. 130-134.

Lehman, J. D. and Yavneh, N. 1985. 'The Total Life Cycle Model,' *Proc. 3rd Int. Workshop Software Specification and Design,* London, pp. 135-137.

Leibrandt, U. and Schnupp, P. 1984. 'An Evaluation of Prolog as a Prototyping System,' *Approaches to Prototyping,* R. Budde, K. Kuhlenkamp, L. Mathiassen and H. Zullighoven (eds.), Berlin: Springer-Verlag, pp. 424-433.

Lenorovitz, D. R. and Ramsey, H. R. 1977. 'A Dialogue Simulation Tool for Use in the Design of Interactive Computer Systems,' *Proc. 21st Annual Meeting of Human Computer Factors Society,* Santa Monica, CA, pp. 95-99.

Levene, A. A. and Mullery, G. P. 1982. 'An Investigation of Requirements Specification Languages: Theory and Practice,' *IEEE Computer,* **15**(1) pp. 50-59.

Levin, D. 1983. 'Programming in SETL Environment,' *Programming Languages and System Design,* J. Bormann (ed.), Amsterdam: North-Holland, pp. 129-137.

Levine, J. 1980. 'Why a Lisp-Based Command Language?,' *SIGPLAN Notices,* **15**(5) pp. 49-53.

Lientz, B. P. 1983. 'Issues in Software Maintenance,' *Computing Surveys,* **15**(3) pp. 271-278.

Lientz, B. P. and Swanson, E. B. 1980. *Software Maintenance Management,* Reading, MA: Addison-Wesley.

Liskov, B. H. and Zilles, S. N. 1975. 'Specification Techniques for Data Abstractions,' *IEEE Trans. Software Engineering,* **1**(1), pp. 7-19.

Litvintchouk, S. D. and Matsumoto, A. S. 1984. 'Design of Ada Systems Using Reusable Components: An Approach Using Structured Algebraic Specification,' *IEEE Trans. Software Engineering,* **10**(5), pp. 544-551.

Luker, P. A. and Burns, A. 1986. 'Program Generators and Generation Software,' *The Computer Journal,* **29**(4) pp. 315-321.

MacEwen, G. H. 1982. 'Specification Prototyping,' *ACM SIGSOFT Software Engineering Notes,* **7**(5) pp. 112-119.

Mallgren, W. R. 1982. 'Formal Specification of Graphic Data Types,' *ACM Trans. Programming Languages and Systems,* **4**(4) pp. 687-710.

Martin, J. 1982. *Application Development Without Programmers,* Englewood Cliffs, NJ: Prentice-Hall.

Mason, R. E. A. and Carey, T. T. 1983. 'Prototyping Interactive Information Systems,' *Communications of the ACM*, **26**(5) pp. 347-354.

Matsumoto, A. S. 1984. 'Some Experience in Promoting Reusable Software Presentation in Higher Abstract Levels,' *IEEE Trans. Software Engineering*, **10**(5) pp. 502-512.

Mayr, H. C., Bever, M. and Lockemann, P. C. 1984. 'Prototyping Interactive Application Systems,' *Approaches to Prototyping*, R. Budde, K. Kuhlenkamp, L. Mathiassen and H. Zullighoven (eds.), Berlin: Springer-Verlag, pp. 105-121.

McCracken, D. D. and Jackson, M. A. 1982. 'Life Cycle Concept Considered Harmful,' *ACM SIGSOFT Software Engineering Notes*, **7**(2) pp. 29-32.

McGowan, C. L., Feblowitz, M. D. and Chandrasekharan, M. 1985. 'The Metafor Approach to Executable Specifications,' *Proc. 3rd Int. Workshop Software Specification and Design*, London, pp. 163-169.

McLean, E. R. 1976. 'The Use of APL for Production Applications: The Concept of Throwaway Code,' *APL 76: Conf. Proc., ACM*.

McNurlin, B. C. 1981. 'Developing Systems by Prototyping,' *EDP Analyzer*, **19**(10), pp. 1-12.

Meandzija, B. 1986. 'A Formal Method for Composing a Network Command Language,' *IEEE Trans. Software Engineering*, **12**(8) pp. 860-865.

Meijer, E. 1979. 'Application Simulation,' *Proc. DESIGN 1979 Symp.*, Monterey, CA, pp. 410-420.

Meyer, B. 1982. 'Principles of Package Design,' *Communications of the ACM*, **25**(7) pp. 419-428.

Meyer, G. J. 1978. *The Art of Software Testing*, New York: Wiley.

Mills, J. A. 1985. 'A Pragmatic View of The System Architect,' *Communications of the ACM*, **28**(7) pp. 708-717.

Minkowitz, C. and Henderson, P. 1986. 'A Formal Description of Object-Oriented Programming Using VDM,' *Tech. Report FPN-13*, Computing Dept., Stirling University.

Mittermeir, R. T. 1982a. 'HIBOL, A Language for Fast Prototyping in Data Processing Environments,' *ACM SIGSOFT Software Engineering Notes* **7**(5) pp. 133-140.

Mittermeir, R. T. 1982b. 'Semantic Nets for Modelling the Requirements of Evolvable Systems – an Example,' *Evolutionary Information Systems*, J. Hawgood (ed.), Amsterdam: North-Holland, pp. 193-216.

Moran, T. P. 1981. 'The Command Language Grammar: A Representation for the User Interface of Interactive Computer Systems,' *Int. Journal of Man–Machine Studies*, **15** pp. 3-50.

Morgan, C. and Sufrin, B. 1984. 'Specification of the UNIX Filing System,' *IEEE Trans. Software Engineering*, **10**(2) pp. 128-142.

Munson, J. B. 1981. 'Software Maintainability: A Practical Concern for Life-Cycle Costs,' *IEEE Computer*, **14**(2) pp. 103-109.

Musser, D. R. 1979. 'Abstract Data Type Specification in the AFFIRM System,' *Proc. Conf. Specification of Reliable Software*, pp. 47-57.

Naumann, J. D. and Jenkins, A. M. 1982. 'Prototyping: The New Paradigm for Systems Development,' *MIS Quarterly*, **10**, pp. 29-44.

Naur, P. *et. al.* 1963. 'Revised Report on the Algorithmic Language Algol 60,' *Comm. of the ACM*, **6**(1), pp. 64-77.

Neighbours, J. M. 1984. 'The Draco Approach to Constructing Software From Reusable Components,' *IEEE Trans. Software Engineering*, **10**(5), pp. 564-578.

Norman, D. A. 1983. 'Design Rules Based on Analysis of Human Error,'*Communications of the ACM*, **26**(4) pp. 254-258.

Nosek, J. T. 1984. 'Organisation Design Choices to Facilitate Evolutionary Development of Prototype Information Systems,' *Approaches to Prototyping*, R. Budde, K. Kuhlenkamp, L. Mathiassen and H. Zullighoven (eds.), Berlin: Springer-Verlag, pp. 341-355.

Parnas, D. L. 1969. 'On The Use of Transition Diagrams in The Design of A User Interface for an Interactive Computer System,' *Proc. 24th Nat. ACM Conf.*, pp. 379-385.

Parnas, D. L. 1972. 'On the Criteria to be Used in Decomposing Systems into Modules,' *Communications of the ACM*, **15**(12) pp. 1053-1058.

Parnas, D. L., Clements, P. C. and Weiss, D. M. 1985. 'The Modular Structure of Complex Systems,' *IEEE Trans. Software Engineering*, **11**(3) pp. 259-272.

Parnas, D. L. and Clements, P. C. 1986. 'A Rational Design Process: How and Why to Fake it,' *IEEE Trans. Software Engineering*, **12**(2) pp. 251-257.

Patton, B. 1983. 'Prototyping – A Nomenclature Problem,' *ACM SIGSOFT Software Engineering Notes*, **8**(2) pp. 14-16.

Podger, D. N. 1979. 'High-Level Languages – A Basis for Participative Design,' *Design and Implementation of Computer-Based Information Systems*, E. Grochla (ed.), Oslo: Sijthoff and Noordhoff.

Polster, F. J. 1986. 'Reuse of Software Through Generation of Partial Systems,' *IEEE Trans. Software Engineering*, **12**(3) pp. 402-416.

Prywes, N. S. and Pnueli, A. 1983. 'Compilation of Nonprocedural Specifications into Computer Programs,' *IEEE Trans. Software Engineering*, **9**(3) pp. 267-279.

Ramamoorthy, C. V., Garg, V. and Prakash, A. 1986. 'Programming in the Large,' *IEEE Trans. Software Engineering*, **12**(7) pp. 769-783.

Ramamoorthy, C. V., Prakash, A., Tsai, W. and Usuda, Y. 1984. 'Software Engineering: Problems and Perspectives,' *IEEE Computer*, **17**(2) pp. 191-209.

Read, N. S. and Harmon, D. L. 1981. 'Assuring MIS Success,' *Datamation*, **27**(2), pp. 109-120.

Rich, C. and Waters, R. C. 1982. 'The Disciplined Use of Simplifying Assumptions,' *ACM SIGSOFT Software Engineering Notes*, **7**(5) pp. 150-154.

Riddle, W. E. 1984. 'Advancing the State of the Art in Software System Prototyping,' *Approaches to Prototyping*, R. Budde, K. Kuhlenkamp, L. Mathiassen and H. Zullighoven (eds.), Berlin: Springer-Verlag, pp. 19-26.

Ross, D. T. and Schoman, K. E. 1977. 'Structured Analysis for Requirements Definition,' *IEEE Trans. Software Engineering*, **3**(1) pp. 6-15.

Rowe, L. A. and Shoens, K. 1983. 'Programming Language Constructs for Screen Definition,' *IEEE Trans. Software Engineering*, **9**(1) pp. 31-39.

Rzevski, G. 1984. 'Prototypes versus Pilot Systems: Strategies for Evolutionary Information System Development,' *Approaches to Prototyping*, R. Budde, K. Kuhlenkamp, L. Mathiassen and H. Zullighoven (eds.), Berlin: Springer-Verlag, pp. 356-367.

Sale, A. E. 1985. 'The Codasyl Proposal for a Screen Management Facility,' *Computer Bulletin*, **1**(1) pp. 24-25.

Sandewall, E. 1978. 'Programming in an Interactive Environment: The Lisp Experience,' *ACM Computing Surveys*, **10**(1) pp. 35-71.

Scott, J. H. 1978. 'The Management Science Opportunity: A Systems Development Management Viewpoint,' *MIS Quarterly*, **2**(4) pp. 59-61.

Shannon, R. E. 1975. *System Simulation – the Art and Science*, Englewood Cliffs, NJ: Prentice-Hall.

Shaw, M. 1985. 'What Can We Specify? Issues in the Domains of Software Specifications,' *Proc. 3rd Int. Workshop Software Specification and Design*, London, pp. 214-215.

Shaw, M., Boriston, E., Horowitz, M., Lane, T., Nichlos, D. and Pausch, R. 1983. 'Descartes: A Programming Language Approach to Information Display Interfaces,' *SIGPLAN Notices*, **18**(6), pp. 100-111

Shneiderman, B. 1979. 'Human Factors Experiments in Designing Interactive Systems,' *IEEE Computer*, **12**(1) pp. 9-19.

Shneiderman, B. 1982. 'Multiparty Grammars and Related Features for Defining Interactive Systems,' *IEEE Trans. Systems, Man and Cybernetics*, **12**(2) pp. 148-154.

Shooman, M. L. 1982. *Software Engineering: Design, Reliability, and Management*, New York: McGraw-Hill.

Silbert, J. L. Hurley, W. D. and Bleser, T. W. 1986. 'An Object-Oriented User Interface Management System,' *SIGGRAPH*, **20**(4) pp. 259-268.

Silverberg, B. A. 1981. 'An Overview of the SRI Hierarchical Development Methodology,' *Software Engineering Environments*, R.Bunke (ed.) , Amsterdam: North-Holland, pp. 235-252.

Smith, D. A. 1982. *Rapid Software Prototyping*, PhD Thesis, University of California, Irvine.

Smith, D. C., Irby, C., Kimball, R. and Verplank, B. 1982. 'Designing the Star User Interface,' *BYTE*, pp. 242-282.

Smith, H. R. and Knuth, C. 1976. 'A Computerized Approach to Systems Analysis: A Technique and its Application,' *Proc. 8th. Annual Conf. American Decision Sciences*, pp. 549-551.

Sol, H. G. 1984. 'Prototyping: A Methodological Assessment,' *Approaches to Prototyping*, R. Budde, K. Kuhlenkamp, L. Mathiassen and H. Zullighoven (eds.), Berlin: Springer-Verlag, pp. 368-382.

Sommerville, I. 1982. *Software Engineering*, Wokingham: Addison-Wesley.

Somogyi, E. K. 1981. 'Prototyping – A Method not to be Missed,' *EDP Analyser*, **19**(10) pp. 114-124.

Stoy, J. 1982. 'Some Mathematical Aspects of Functional Programming,' *Functional Programming and its Applications*, J. Darlington, P. Henderson and D. Turner (eds.), Cambridge: Cambridge University Press, pp. 217-252.

Sufrin, B. 1982. 'Formal Specification of a Display-Oriented Text Editor,' *Science of Computer Programming*, **1**, pp. 157-202.

Sufrin, B. 1986. 'Formal Methods and the Design of Effective User Interfaces,' *People and Computers: Designing for Usability*, M. D. Harrison and A. I. Monk (eds.), Cambridge: Cambridge University Press, pp. 24-43.

Sunshine, C. A., Thompson, D. H., Erickson, R. W., Gerhart, S. L. and Schwabe, D. 1982. 'Specification and Verification of Communication Protocols in AFFIRM Using State Transition Models,' *IEEE Trans. Software Engineering*, **8**(5) pp. 460-489.

Sutton, J. A. and Sprague, R. H. 1978. 'A Study of Display Generation and Management in Interactive Business Applications,' *IBM Research Rep. RJ2392*.

Swanson, E. B. 1976. 'The Dimensions of Maintenance,' *Proc. 2nd Int. Conf. Software Engineering*, Munich, pp. 492-497.

Swartout, W. and Balzer, R. 1982. 'On the Inevitable Intertwining of Specification and Implementation,' *Communications of the ACM*, **25**(7) pp. 438-440.

Taggart, W. M. and Tharp, M. O. 1977. 'A Survey of Information Requirements Analysis Techniques,' *Computing Surveys*, **9**(4) pp. 271-289.

Tavendale, R. D. 1985. 'A Technique for Prototyping Directly from a Specification,' *Proc. 8th Int. Conf. Software Engineering*, London, pp. 224-229.

Tavolato, P. and Vincena, K. 1984. 'A Prototyping Methodology and its Tools,' *Approaches to Prototyping*, R. Budde, K. Kuhlenkamp, L. Mathiassen and H. Zullighoven (eds.), Berlin: Springer-Verlag, pp. 434-446.

Teichroew, D. and Hershey, E. A. 1977. 'PSL/PSA: A Computer-Aided Technique for Structured Documentation and Analysis of Information Processing Systems,' *IEEE Trans. Software Engineering*, **3**(1) pp. 41-48.

Teitelman, W. 1979. 'A Display Oriented Programmer's Assistant,' *Int. Journal of Man–Machine Studies*, **11** pp. 157-187.

Ten Hagen, P. J. W. 1980. 'A Conceptual Basis for Graphical Input and Output Interaction,' *Methodology of Interaction*, R. A. Guedj *et al.* (eds.), Amsterdam: North-Holland, pp. 239-246.

Ten Hagen, P. J. W. and Dresken, J. 1985. 'Parallel Input and Feedback in Dialogue Cells,' *UIMS*, G. E. Pfaff (ed.), Berlin: Springer-Verlag, pp. 109-124.

Tomeski, E. A. and Lazarus, H. 1975. *People-oriented Computer Systems*, New York: Van Nostrand Reinhold.

Tseng, J. S., Szymanski, B., Shi, Y. and Prywes, N. S. 1986. 'Real-Time Software Life Cycle with the Model System,' *IEEE Trans. Software Engineering*, **12**(2) pp. 358-373.

Tsichritzis, D. 1980. 'OFS: An Integrated Form Management System,' *Proc. ACM Conf. Very Large Data Bases*, pp. 190-194.

Tsichritzis, D. 1982. 'Form Management,' *Communications of the ACM*, **25**(7) pp. 453-478.

Turner, D. A. 1979. 'A New Implementation Technique for Applicative Languages,' *Software Practice and Experience*, **9**(1), pp. 31-49.

Turner, D. A. 1985. *Miranda: A Non-Strict Functional Language with Polymorphic Types*, Lecture Notes in Computer Science, **201**, Berlin: Springer-Verlag.

Turoff, M., Hiltz, S. R. and Kerr, E. B. 1982. 'Controversies in the Design of Computer-Mediated Communication Systems: A Delphi Study,' *Proc. Conf. Human Factors in Computer Systems*, Gaithersburg, Maryland, pp. 89-100.

Urban, J. E. 1982. 'Software Development with Executable Functional Specifications,' *Proc. 6th. Int. Conf. Software Engineering*, Tokyo, Japan, pp. 418-419.

Van Hoeve, F. A. and Engmann, R. 1984. 'The TUBA–Project: A Set of Tools for Application Development and Prototyping,' *Approaches to Prototyping*, R. Budde, K. Kuhlenkamp, L. Mathiassen and H. Zullighoven (eds.), Berlin: Springer-Verlag, pp. 202-213.

Van Meurs, J. and Cardozo, E.L. 1977. 'Interfacing the User', *Software Practice and Experience*, **7**(1) pp. 85-93.

Venken, R. and Bruynooghe, M. 1984. 'Prolog as a Language for Prototyping of Information Systems,' *Approaches to Prototyping*, R. Budde, K. Kuhlenkamp, L. Mathiassen and H. Zullighoven (eds.), Berlin: Springer-Verlag, pp. 447-458.

Wang, M. D. 1970. 'The Rule of Syntactic Complexity as a Determinator of Comprehensibility,' *Journal Verbal Learning and Verbal Behaviour*, **9** pp. 398-404.

Wasserman, A. I. 1985. 'Extending State Transition Diagrams for the Specification of Human–Computer Interaction,' *IEEE Trans. Software Engineering*, **11**(8) pp. 699-713.

Wasserman, A. I. and Shewmake, D. T. 1982a. 'Automating the Development and Evolution of User Dialogue in an Interactive Information System,' *Evolutionary Information Systems*, J. Hawgood (ed.), Amsterdam: North-Holland, pp. 159-172.

Wasserman, A. I. and Shewmake, D. T. 1982b. 'Rapid Prototyping of Interactive Information Systems,' *ACM SIGSOFT Software Engineering Notes*, **7**(5) pp. 171-180.

Wasserman, A. I. and Stinson, S. K. 1979. 'A Specification Method for Interactive Information Systems,' *Proc. Conf. Specification of Reliable Software*, pp. 68-79.

Waters, S. J. 1979. 'Towards Comprehensive Specifications,' *The Computer Journal*, **22**(3) pp. 195-199.

Weber, H. and Ehrig, H. 1986. 'Specification of Modular Systems,' *IEEE Trans. Software Engineering*, **12**(7) pp. 784-798.

Webster, R. and Miner, M. 1983. 'Apple Lisa,' *Personal Computer World*, **6**(7), pp. 146-159.

Weiser, M. 1982. 'Scale Models and Rapid Prototyping,' *ACM SIGSOFT Software Engineering Notes*, **7**(5) pp. 181-185.

Weyuker, E. J. 1982. 'On Testing Non-Testable Programs,' *Computer Journal*, **25**(4), pp. 465-470.

Wilensky, R. 1984. *LISPcraft*, New York: Norton.

Winston, P. H. and Horn, B. K. P. 1981. *Lisp*, Reading, MA: Addison-Wesley.

Yao, S. B., Hevner, A. R., Shi, A. and Luo, D. 1984. 'FORMANAGER: An Office Forms Management System,' *ACM Trans. Office Information Systems*, **2**(3), pp. 235-262.

Young, R. M. 1981. 'The Machine Inside the Machine: User's Models of Pocket Calculators,' *Int. Journal of Man–Machine Studies*, **15**, pp. 51-58.

Zave, P. and Schell, W. 1986. 'Salient Features of an Executable Specification Language and Its Environment,' *IEEE Trans. Software Engineering*, **12**(2) pp. 312-325.

Zelkowitz, M. V. 1980. 'A Case Study in Rapid Prototyping,' *Software Practice and Experience*, **10** pp. 1037-1042.

Zelkowitz, M. V. 1984. 'A Taxonomy of Prototype Designs,' *ACM SIGSOFT Software Engineering Notes*, **9**(5) pp. 11-12.

Zelkowitz, M. V., Shaw, A. C. and Gannon, J. D. 1979. *Principles of Software Engineering and Design*, Englewood Cliffs, NJ: Prentice-Hall.

Appendix A
EPROS Reference Manual

A.1 EPROL syntax

A formal definition of the syntax of EPROL follows. It is specified in extended BNF: [...] specifies optional constructs, {...}* specifies zero or more repetitions, {...}+ specifies one or more repetitions, and | specifies choice. Non-terminal appear in Times Roman, and terminals appear in a different font.

Prototype ::=
    [Const-def] [Dom-def] [Type-def] [Aux-def] {Adt-def}* [Design-def]
Const-def ::=
    CONST {Identifier = Expression ; }+
Dom-def ::=
    DOM {Abs-syn-rule ; }+
Adt-def ::=
    ADT Identifier Dom-def [Type-def] [Aux-def] Ops-def END Identifier
Type-def ::=
    TYPE {Fun-type-def ; }+
Aux-def ::=
    AUX [Inv-body-def ;] {Fun-body-def ; }*
Ops-def ::=
    OPS {Operation-def}+
Fun-type-def ::=
    Identifier : [Domain {, Domain}*] $\rightarrow$ Domain
Fun-body-def ::=
    Identifier Parameter-list $\triangleq$ Expression ;
Inv-body-def ::=
    inv- Fun-body-def

Operation-def ::=
  Identifier : Op-type-clause ;
  [pre- Parameter-list ≙ Expression ; | exep- Parameter-list ≙ Exep-list ;]
  post- Parameter-list ≙ Expression ; {Fun-def-body ; }* END Identifier
Op-type-clause ::=
  [Domain {, Domain}*] → [Domain]
Exep-list ::=
  Expression → String {, Expression → String}*
Parameter-list ::=
  ([(Identifier | Tree-par) {, (Identifier | Tree-par)}*])
Tree-par ::=
  (Identifier {, Identifier}+)
Abs-syn-rule ::=
  Identifier (= (Simple-domain | Domain) | :: Tree-domain)
Tree-domain ::=
  S-Domain {, S-domain}+
S-domain ::=
  . Identifier : Domain
Simple-domain ::=
  { (Int-const {, Int-const}*) | (Int-const : Int-const) |
   (Char-const {, Char-const}*) | (Char-const : Char-const) }
Domain ::=
  Identifier | Elementary-set | Str | File | (Domain (-set | -list)) |
  (Domain → Domain) | ((Domain)) | ([Domain]) |
  (Domain {| Domain}+) | (tree Tree-domain) |
  (array {[Expression]}+ Domain) | (form Identifier) | (Domain -dbase)|
  {*}+
Elementary-set ::=
  Bool | Nat | Nat0 | Int | Real | Char
Expression ::=
  (Simple-expr {(= | ≠ | > | < | ⟩ | ⟨ | ∧ | ∨ | ∈ | ⊂ | ⊆ | ⇒ | ⇔) Simple-expr}+) |
  If-expr | Mac-expr | Cases-expr | Let-expr
Simple-expr ::=
  ([+ | -] Term {(† | ∘ | ∪ | - | +) Term}*) |
  (((mk- Identifier) | mk) (Expression {, Expression}+))
Term ::=
  Factor {(⁓ | ◁ | ◀ | ∩ | ^ | % | / | *) Factor}*
Factor ::=
  Constant | Identifier | (Identifier (Expression {, Expression}*))
  | (Expression) | ((card | power | len | hd | tl | elems | inds | conc | dom |
  rng | merge | ∪ | @ | ¬) Factor) |
  (Factor (. Identifier | [Expression] | (Expression))) |
  Quantification | Set-enumeration | list-enumeration | mapping-enumeration |
  Map-factor | Dist-factor | Text
Map-factor ::=

    map ((Identifier I Unary-operator I Binary-operator)

    {, (Identifier I Unary-operator I Binary-operator)}* : Expression)

Dist-factor ::=

    dist ((Identifier I Binary-operator I Binary-lambda)

    {, (Identifier I Binary-operator I Binary-lambda)}* : Expression)

Binary-lambda ::=

    λ Identifier , Identifier Expression

Text ::=

    \ {Character}* \

Quantification ::=

    (ι Identifier I ι! Identifier I (($\forall$ I $\exists$ I $\exists$!) Identifier {, Identifier}*))

    $\in$ Expression : Expression)

Let-expr ::=

    let (Identifier I (Identifier {, Identifier}+)) = Expression

    {, (Identifier I (Identifier {, Identifier}+)) = Expression}* **in** Expression

If-expr ::=

    if Expression **then** Expression **else** Expression

Mac-expr ::=

    mac (Expression $\rightarrow$ Expression {, Expression $\rightarrow$ Expression}+)

Cases-expr ::=

    cases Expression

    (Expression $\rightarrow$ Expression {, (Expression I TRUE) $\rightarrow$ Expression}+)

Set-enumeration ::=

    Explicit-set-enum I Implicit-set-enum

Explicit-set-enum ::=

    { [Expression {, Expression}*] I Expression : Expression }

Implicit-set-enum ::=

    { Expression : Expression }

List-enum ::=

    Explicit-list-enum I Implicit-list-enum

Explicit-list-enum ::=

    < [Expression {, Expression}*] >

Implicit-list-enum ::=

    < Expression : Expression >

Mapping-enum ::=

    Explicit-mapping-enum I Implicit-mapping-enum

Explicit-mapping-enum ::=

    [[Expression $\mapsto$ Expression {, Expression $\mapsto$ Expression}*]]

Implicit-mapping-enum ::=

    [Expression $\mapsto$ Expression : Expression]

Design-def ::=

    DESIGN Identifier Ifunction-head ; Block Identifier

Ifunction-head ::=

    ([[VAR] Identifier : Domain {, [VAR] Identifier : Domain}*]) [: Domain]

Block ::=

[Dem-def] [Var-def] {Forward-def}* {Module-def}* Ifunction-body
Var-def ::=
    VAR {Identifier {, Identifier}* : Domain [:= Expression] ; }+
Forward-def ::=
    FORWARD Identifier ([[VAR] Domain {, [VAR] Domain}*]) [: Domain] ;
Module-def ::=
    Ifunction-def I Dialogue-def I Form-def I Cluster-def
Ifunction-body ::=
    BEGIN Statement {; Statement} END
Ifunction-def ::=
    FUNCTION Identifier Ifunction-head ; Block Identifier
Dialogue-def ::=
    DIALOGUE Identifier ; [Dom-def] [Var-def]
    {Forward-def}* {Module-def}* Dialogue-body Identifier
Dialogue-body ::=
    BEGIN
    {state Identifier : Statement → Dial-state ; I
    iap Identifier : Statement ; {: Expression {, Statement}* → Dial-state ;
    }+}+
    END
Dial-state ::=
    Identifier I (return [(Expression)])
Form-def ::=
    FORM Identifier Text {Field-def}+ END Identifier
Field-def ::=
    $identifier : Field-type {, Field-attribute}* ;
Field-type ::=
    Identifier (Nat-const)
Field-attribute ::=
    system Identifier I constraint Expression I initially Expression I
    computed Statement I ((after I lock) [($identifier {, $identifier}*)]) I
    required I permanent I optional I noecho
Cluster ::=
    CLUSTER Identifier { Cluster-scheme } [: Domain] ; Cluster-body Identifier
Cluster-scheme ::=
    { Identifier : ((Const I Ident I Expr) : Domain I Statm) I
     ' Literal ' I
    (Cluster-scheme) I
    (Cluster-scheme { I Cluster-scheme}+) Identifier I
    [Cluster-scheme] Identifier I
    { Cluster-scheme } (* Identifier I + Identifier I Nat-const) }+
Cluster-body ::=
    BEGIN {(Statement I on-exit do Statement) ; }+ END
Statement ::=
    [Identifier :]

    if Expression **then** Statement [**else** Statement] |
    Mac-stat | cases-stat | **while** Expression **do** Statement |
    do Statement **while** Expression | **for** Identifier **in** Expression **do** Statement |
    Identifier ([Expression {, Expression}*]) |
    Identifier {(Expression) | [Expression] | . Identifier}* := Expression
    Cluster-call | **assert** Expression | **goto** Identifier | **return** [Expression] |
    done | Compound-stat | Put-stat | Get-stat | Menu-stat | Switch-stat
Mac-stat ::=
    mac { Expression → Expression {; Expression → Expression}+ }
Cases-stat ::=
    cases Expression
    { Expression → Expression {; (Expression | TRUE) → Expression}+ }
Cluster-call ::=
    Identifier { {Expression | Literal | Statement}* }
Literal ::=
    {Character}+
Compound-stat ::=
    { Statement {; Statement}* }
Put-stat ::=
    put ([Identifier ,] string {, Expression}*)
Get-stat ::=
    get ([Identifier , | String ,] Identifier {, Identifier}*)
Menu-stat ::=
    menu { String {(String | TRUE) [, **constraint** Expression] → Statement
    ;}+}
Switch-stat ::=
    switch { String
    {(((String [, **constraint** Expression] , **tick** Expression) |
      (TRUE [, **constraint** Expression] → Statement)) ;}+ }
Constant ::=
    Int-const | Real-const | Char-const | Str-const | TRUE | FALSE | NIL
Int-const ::=
    [+ | −] Nat-const
Real-const ::=
    (Int-const . [Nat-const] [E Int-const]) | (Int-const E Int-const)
Nat-const ::=
    {Digit}+
Char-const ::=
    ' Character '
Identifier ::=
    Alpha {Alpha | Digit}* {'}*
$identifier ::=
    $ Identifier
Alpha ::=
    a | b | c | ... | z | A | B | C | ... | _

Digit ::=
          0 | 1 | 2 | 3 | 4 | 5 | 6 | 7 | 8 | 9
Character ::=
          any visible character

A.2   ASCII equivalents

The operators used in this book are represented by a set of ASCII characters in
EPROL, as illustrated by the diagram below. Obviously, when using the tool, the
ASCII equivalents should be used instead.

	&	⊂	. P .
∧	|	⊆	. S .
∨		᷉	| |
¬	~	◁	/ +
⇒	= = >	◀	/ −
⇔	< = >	†	+ +
∀	. A	∘	^
∃	. E	^	* *
∃!	. E !	≢	/ =
⍳	!	≜	= =
⍳!	! !	↦	− >
∈	#	→	− >
∪	. U .	→	= >
∩	. I .	→	-->
∪	union		

A.3   Standard libraries

Five standard libraries of EPROL are described. The use of each library must be
explicitly stated using a library directive (e.g., *%library* "scr").

A.3.1   The maths library: math

exp: Real → Real;
exp(x)
          Returns the number e raised to the power of x.

log: Real → Real;
log(x)
          Returns the (base e) logarithm of x.

fix: Real → Int;
fix(x)
> Returns the integral part of x.

float: Int → Real;
float(i)
> Converts i to a real number.

abs: Int | Real → Int | Real;
abs(n)
> Returns the absolute value of n.

sqrt: Int | Real → Real;
sqrt(n)
> Returns the square root of n.

sin: Real → Real;
sin(x)
> Returns the sine of angle x.

cos: Real → Real;
cos(x)
> Returns the cosine of angle x.

evenp: Int → Bool;
evenp(i)
> Returns TRUE if i is an even number, and FALSE otherwise.

oddp: Int → Bool;
oddp(i)
> Returns TRUE if i is an odd number, and FALSE otherwise.

A.3.2   The string library: str

st_new: Nat0 → Str;
st_new(i)
> Returns a new string which initially contains i blanks.

st_len: Str → Nat0;
st_len(s)
> Returns the length (i.e., the number of characters) of s.

st_app: Str, Str → Str;
st_app(s1,s2)
> Returns a new string which is the result of appending s2 to s1.

st_left: Nat0, Str → Str;
st_left(i,s)
> Returns a new string which consists of the i leftmost characters of s.

st_right: Nat0, Str → Str;
st_right(i,s)
> Returns a new string which consists of the i rightmost characters of s.

st_mid: Nat0, Nat0, Str → Str;
st_mid(i,j,s)
> Returns a new string which consists of the ith through the jth character of s.

st_mk: Char-list → Str;
st_mk(cl)
> Returns a new string which consists of the characters in list cl.

st_unmk: Str → Char-list;
st_unmk(s)
> Returns a list of all characters in s.

A.3.3   The I/O library: io

f_open (f: Str, m: Str): File;
> Opens and returns a file with name f and mode m; m may be one of "r " (for reading), "w" (for writing), "r+w" (for reading and writing), or "a" (for appending).

f_close (f: File);
> Closes file f.

f_getc (f: File): Char;
> Reads and returns the next character of file f.

f_getl (f: File): Str;
> Reads and returns the next line of file f.

f_zap (file: File);
> Reads and ignores to the end of the current line of file f.

f_copy (f1: *Str*, f2: *Str*);
> Copies the contents of file f1 to file f2.

unix (com: *Str*): *Int*;
> Executes com as a UNIX command and returns the status as an integer.

inp
> Standard input.

outp
> Standard output.

EOF
> End of file marker.

A.3.4   The screen library: scr

init_scr ();
> Initializes and clears the VDU screen and forces the terminal into special mode for screen I/O. The cursor is moved to the top left hand corner of the screen. This function must be called before any other function in the scr library.

tini_scr ();
> Performs the reverse of init_scr by restoring the original modes of the terminal.

clear ();
> Clears the VDU screen.

move (lin: *Nat*, col: *Nat*);
> Moves the cursor to the coordinates (lin,col). If this lies outside the screen then it will be automatically adjusted to the nearest position inside the screen.

w_open (lins: *Nat*, cols: *Nat*, titl: *Str*);
> Opens a window with its origin positioned at the current position of the cursor. The window will be lins lines long and cols columns wide. The title titl will be displayed on top of the window. If the window, or part of it, lies outside the screen then its position will be automatically adjusted to the nearest suitable position. A window larger than the entire screen will be reduced to the size of the screen.

w_close (n: *Nat0*);
> Closes the n most recently opened windows in the reverse order of opening. The cursor will be moved back to its original position, i.e., where it was before the window was opened

w_move (lin: *Nat*, col: *Nat*);
> Moves the cursor to the local coordinates (lin,col) inside the current window. If the position lies outside the window then it will be automatically adjusted to the nearest position inside the window.

w_clear ();
> Clears the contents of the current window. The cursor will be moved to the top left hand corner of the window.

w_scroll (n: *Int*);
> This function first awaits the press of a key (any key will do). It will then scroll the current window by n lines. A negative n specifies the number of lines of the old text to be kept after a scroll. If n is zero then the window will be scrolled h-1 lines where h is the height of the window.

w_text (lins: *Nat*, cols: *Nat*, titl: *Str*, tex: *File | Strlist*);
> This function first opens a window of the specified size and title (see w_open), and then displays tex in the window. Tex may be a text file or a string list. The window may be scrolled as many times as necessary to accommodate the whole text. Once the entire text is displayed the window will be closed upon pressing any key.

w_spec (spec: *Char*): *Int*;
> This function may be used to obtain the specification of current window according to the following values for spec:
> 'L' – length of window.
> 'C' – height of window.
> 'l' – origin line of window.
> 'c' – origin column of window.

bell ();
> Rings the margin bell.

keybd ();
> Returns the next key stroke.

wait (n: *Nat0*);
> Waits for n seconds.

time (t: *Char*): *Int*;
> Returns the current time according to the following values for t:

> 'Y' – year
> 'M' – month
> 'D' – day
> 'h' – hour
> 'm' – minute
> 's' – second

fm_new (f: *Form* *, titl: *Str*);
> Displays the form f in a window having the title titl. The user is then
> invited to fill the form interactively.

fm_view (f: *Form* *, titl: *Str*);
> Displays the form f in a window having the title titl. The specification of
> the window is deduced from the form itself.

fm_drain (f: *Form* *);
> Drains the image of the form f.

fm_put (file: *File*, f: *Form* *);
> Writes the image of the form f to file.

fm_get (file: *File*, f: *Form* *);
> Reads the image of the form f from file.

A.3.5   The database library: dbase

db_init (db: *-*dbase*);
> Initializes the database db.

db_size (db: *-*dbase*): *Nat0*;
> Returns the size (i.e., the number of records) of db.

db_insert (db: *-*dbase*, rec: *): *Bool*;
> Inserts the record rec into database db provided it is not already there. A
> successful insertion will return TRUE; a failure will return FALSE.

db_delete (db: *-*dbase*, k: **): *Bool*;
> Deletes the record whose key matches k from db provided it is already in the
> database. If successful it will return TRUE, otherwise it will return FALSE.

db_find (db: *-*dbase*, k: **): * | *NIL*;
> Finds and returns the record in db whose key matches k. If no record with
> such key exists then NIL will be returned.

db_list (db: *-*dbase*): *-*list*;
> Returns a list of records in db.

A.4   Using EPROS

The EPROS system is designed as a software development environment. As a result, a user of the system should be able to do all his work within the environment without actually going back to the operating system. The user interacts with the system through a simple command language that allows him to do day to day work such as editing, compiling and printing files, invoking EPROS tools, sending commands to and receiving messages from the operating system, etc.

This section describes aspects which should be of interest to those who use the system. In particular it describes the command language, the interpreter, the compiler, the executer and the tools available in the environment. The examples in this section are based on a simple EPROL file called myfile.e, the contents of which is shown below.

```
ADT Stack
   DOM Stack = Int-list;
   OPS
     INIT: → ;
        post(st,st') ≙ st' = <>;
     END INIT

     PUSH: Int → ;
        post(st,i,st') ≙ st' = <i> ⁀ st;
     END PUSH

     POP: → ;
        pre(st) ≙ st ≠ <>;
        post(st,st') ≙ st' = tl st;
     END POP
END Stack
```

A.4.1   The command level

EPROS is invoked by typing the command eps. UNIX will then load and run the system (this should take a few seconds):

```
$ eps
[EPROS 1.13, Nov-86]
>>
```

where $ is the UNIX prompt and >> is the EPROS prompt. The prompt indicates that the user is at the **command level**: the user may send his requests to the system by typing appropriate commands. If a request is a valid one the system will execute it, otherwise it will produce an error message. In either case, once the request is handled the system will come up with the prompt >> indicating that it is ready to execute the next command. Each command is briefly described below.

ec   compile an EPROL file.
        Example:
        `ec myfile.e`
ed   edit a file.
        Example:
        `ed myfile.e`
ei   interpret an intermediate or object file.
        Example:
        `ei myfile.l`
h   give general help (a list of commands).
        Example:
        `h`
hi   highlight an EPROL file.
        Example:
        `hi myfile.e`
ld   load an intermediate or object file.
        Example:
        `ld myfile.l`
op   optimize an intermediate file.
        Example:
        `op myfile.l`
pr   print a file.
        Example:
        `pr myfile.l`
q   quit the system.
        Example:
        `q`
xref   produce cross reference for an EPROL file.
        Example:
        `xref myfile.e`
!   execute a UNIX command, or temporarily escape to UNIX.
        Example:
        `!ls -l myfile.e`
?   give synopsis on a subject.
        Example:
        `?xref`
??   give help on a subject.
        Example:
        `??xref`

A.4.2 The compiler

The EPROL compiler is part of the EPROS environment and runs within it. Apart from compiling files, it also updates the symbol table; this is usually used by the interpreter. The command for compiling a file is `ec`. For example, to compile `myfile.e` we may type:

```
>> ec myfile.e
```

The compiler will respond with the message:

```
myfile.e -ec-> myfile.l
-- no errors
-- no warnings
>>
```

The first line shows the source and the target files. It indicates that the compiler takes an EPROL file (always ending in `.e`) and produces an intermediate target file (always ending in `.l`). The next two lines indicate that the file is compiled successfully with no errors or warnings. The compiler always assumes that the source file is a `.e` file. So, typing

```
>> ec myfile
```

will have the same effect.

There are a number of useful options associated with the compiler. An option is specified by a minus symbol followed by a letter representing the option. For example,

```
>> ec -q myfile
```

will compile `myfile.e` in *quiet* mode. The following options are available.

d   Autoload the target file after successful compilation. The autoloaded file will be a `.o` file if the M option is also present, otherwise it will be a `.l` file.

m   Treat the source file as a collection of modules. This option is used for separate compilation, e.g.:

```
>> ec -m myfile
myfile.e -ec-> myfile.l, myfile.m
```

M   Compile into machine code. This will produce a `.o` file.

p   Ignore pre-conditions. The pre-conditions for functions and operations will be compiled as usual but ignored during execution.

q   Compile in quiet mode. This will suppress all compiler messages except errors and warnings.

t   Produce a compiler listing of the source file. The compiler listing will be stored in a .t file, e.g.,

```
>> ec -t myfile
myfile.e -ec-> myfile.l, myfile.t
```

where myfile.t is the compiler listing file.

w   Suppress warning messages.

When more than one option is used it may be expressed in two different ways. For example,

```
>> ec -qtd myfile
```

is equivalent to

```
>> ec -q -t -d myfile
```

and compiles myfile.e in quiet mode, produces compiler listing, and autoloads the target file.

A.4.3   Separate compilation

A system may be broken down into a number of files where each file is compiled separately. This is done using the m option of the compiler. For example, to separately compile a file called part1.e we may type:

```
>> ec -m part1
```

When the m option is used the compiler produces a .m file besides the usual files. This file may be used by other files using a module directive (see below). This feature is useful for large systems or a collection of modules which are commonly used by a number of files.

A.4.4   Compiler directives

There are three compiler directives which may be used in an EPROL file. Each directive is specified by a % (at the beginning of a line) followed by the directive name, followed by its argument. The directives are:

```
%include "filename"
%library "libraryname"
%module  "filename.m"
```

The first directive takes a file and textually includes it within the source file. For example, if

```
%include "myfile1"
```

appears in myfile.e then the compiler will include the contents of myfile1 in myfile.e at the point where the directive appears. This, of course, will not affect the contents of myfile.e; rather it indicates the way the compiler will see the source file.

The module directive is used in association with the m option. Suppose myfile.e makes use of the modules in two other files called myfile1.e and myfile2.e which have been compiled separately. The following directives should appear in myfile.e at some point before the modules are actually used.

```
%module "myfile1.m"
%module "myfile2.m"
```

The library directive informs the compiler that modules of some specified library have been referenced. For example,

```
%library "scr"
```

specifies that the scr library has been used by the file in which it appears.

The include and module directives may be nested to any depth. The library directive, however, may not be nested.

A.4.5   The interpreter

The interpreter is invoked by the ei command and interprets the intermediate code generated by the compiler. For example, to interpret myfile.e one should type:

```
>> ec myfile
>> ei myfile
```

Here myfile.e is first compiled into myfile.l and then loaded by the interpreter. The interpreter can also be run on its own, in which case it acts as an interactive language. To run it on its own one should simply type:

```
>> ei
```

The interpreter supports two modes: the **expression** mode and the **statement** mode, identified by the prompts expr > and stat>, respectively. The first mode is the default mode, i.e., each time the interpreter is invoked it will be initially in this mode. To switch between the modes the user should type a backquote character:

```
>> ei
expr> `
stat> `
expr>
```

In the expr mode the interpreter repeatedly reads, evaluates and prints the value of expressions. Any valid EPROL expression may be given. Here are a few examples:

```
expr> 10;
10
expr> 10*2.5-2;
23
expr> {i: i ∈ {1:10} ∧ i%2 = 0};
{2,4,6,8,10}
expr>
```

Note that each expression should end with a semicolon. An expression may be more than one line long, e.g.:

```
expr> let s = {5,10},
--&->      t = {20,10} in
--&->      s ∪ t;
{5,10,20}
expr>
```

The prompt --&-> indicates that the system expects more input to complete the expression.

In the stat mode the system repeatedly reads and executes statements. Here are a few examples:

```
stat> put("this is a string^n");
this is a string
stat> ppr({1:10})
{1:10}
stat>
```

Again, each statement must end with a semicolon. As with expressions, a statement may be many lines long, e.g.:

```
stat> for i in {1:4} do
--&->      put("%d, %d^n",i,i**2);
1,  1
2,  4
3,  9
4,  16
stat>
```

Errors and warnings reported by the interpreter are identical to those reported by the compiler. Here is an example:

```
stat> for i {1:4} do
*EI_____1
          1: ERROR 135, 'in' expected.
```

The use of the backquote character for switching between the expr and stat modes was mentioned earlier. It can also be used to indicate that what follows must be executed in the other mode. For example, in

```
expr> `ppr({});
{}
expr>
```

the backquote indicates that ppr({}) must be executed as a statement. The interpreter will remain in the expr mode after the execution. Similarly, in

```
stat> `10 + 20;
30
stat>
```

the backquote indicates that 10 must be treated as an expression and not a statement. The use of backquote in this way is handy when we wish to remain in one mode but occasionally refer to the other mode without actually changing the mode. The commands understood by the interpreter are summarized below.

q	Quit the interpreter and go back to the command level.
!	UNIX command or temporary escape to UNIX.
?	Give synopsis on a subject.
??	Give help on a subject.
@	Interrogate the symbol table.
@@	Remove an object from the symbol table.
DOM	Domain definition.
TYPE	Type definition.
AUX	Auxiliary function definition.
VAR	Variable definition.

A.4.6 Defining things

The user can define the following when interacting with the interpreter:

- Domains
- Type clauses
- Auxiliary functions
- Variables

These are defined in much the same way as they are defined when writing EPROL programs. We shall describe the differences through a few examples. The following apply to both the expr and stat mode. In the examples, however, we shall use the expr mode. An example of a domain definition is given below.

```
expr> DOM m = Int → Str;;
expr>
```

It defines m to be the domain of mappings from Int to Str. Note that the definition ends with two semicolons rather than one. This feature allows us to define more than one domain using a single DOM command, e.g.:

```
expr> DOM m = D1 → D2;
--&->     D1 = Int-list;
--&->     D2 = D1-list;;
expr>
```

As shown above, the interpreter expects more domain definitions until a definition ends with a double semicolon. The same rule applies to variables:

```
expr> VAR x: D1;
--&->     y: m;;
expr>
```

An auxiliary function is defined by first defining its type clause using a TYPE command and then the function itself using the AUX command, e.g.:

```
expr> TYPE max: Int-list → Int;;
expr> AUX pre-max(il) ≙ il ≠ <>;
--&->     max(il)≙(ι i ∈ elems il: (∀ j ∈ elems il: i⩾j));;
expr>
```

Again the TYPE and AUX commands, just like the DOM and VAR commands, allow the definition of more than one type clause or function, with the last definition ending with a double semicolon. All definitions given to the interpreter are readily executable. For example:

```
expr> max(<5,10,20,2,1>);
20
expr>
```

A.4.7   Examining definitions

The command @ allows the user to find out what is currently defined. For example,

```
expr> @Bool
Bool    dom     {TRUE,FALSE}
expr>
```

examines the definition of Bool. The system responds by saying that Bool is a domain defined as {TRUE,FALSE}. The @ command can be used with any identifier. For example, given the definition of the max function above, we have:

```
expr> @max
max    fun    Int-list → Int
expr>
```

It can also be used in association with the following classes.

```
CONST       DOM         TYPE        AUX
ADT         OPS         VAR         FUNCTION
DIALOGUE    FORWARD     CLUSTER
```

For example, given the definition in section A.4, we have:

```
expr> @ADT
ABSTRACT DATA TYPES:
Stack  Int-list
expr> @OPS
OPERATIONS:
INIT   [Int-list]
       →
PUSH   [Int-list]
       Int →
POP    [Int-list]
       →
expr>
```

Alternatively, @ on its own will list all the definitions currently known to the system (this usually produces a long list and is not shown here). @ uses the following abbreviations for objects.

`const`	constants
`dom`	domains
`fun?`	function (only type clause defined)
`fun`	function (fully defined)
`adt`	abstract data type
`op`	operation
`var`	variable
`imp`	bound variable
`ifun?`	imperative function (forward reference)
`ifun`	imperative function (fully defined)
`dial?`	dialogue (forward reference)
`dial`	dialogue (fully defined)
`form`	form
`clus`	cluster

The command `@@` removes definitions from the system. It may be used in one of three ways. When used with an identifier it just removes the definition of that identifier, e.g.:

```
expr> @max
max      fun    Int-list → Int
expr> @@max
expr> @max
'max' is not defined.
expr>
```

Alternatively, it may be used on its own, in which case it removes all the definitions given to the system at the interpreter level:

```
expr> @@
all temporary definitions removed.
expr>
```

Finally, the keyword `all` may be used to request the removal of everything, even those produced by the compiler, e.g.:

```
expr> @@all
all definitions removed.
expr>
```

A.4.8   The highlighter

The highlighter takes an EPROL file and prints it on the screen. It highlights the keywords in the file by printing them in bold. An example is shown below.

```
>> hi myfile
ADT Stack
  DOM Stack = Int-list;
  OPS
    INIT: → ;
      post(st,st') ≙ st' = <>;
    END INIT

    PUSH: Int → ;
      post(st,i,st') ≙ st' = <i> ⁀ st;
    END PUSH

    POP: → ;
      pre(st) ≙ st ≠ <>;
      post(st,st') ≙ st' = tl st;
    END POP
END Stack
>>
```

The highlighter assumes that the input file is a **.e** file. It is useful for looking at the contents of a file to make sure that the keywords are properly spelled and that the text is properly indented.

A.4.9   The optimizer

The intermediate code generated by the compiler can be submitted to an optimizer for improvement. For example,

```
>> ec -q myfile
>> op myfile
```

compiles and optimizes myfile. The optimizer assumes that its input file is a **.l** file.

A.4.10   The cross referencer

The cross referencer produces cross references for EPROL files. A cross reference lists all identifiers in a file together with the line numbers in which they appear. For example,

```
>> xref myfile
```

will produce `myfile.x` which contains the following.

```
IDENTIFIER    LINE NUMBER
==========    ===========
INIT           4    6
POP           12   15
PUSH           8   10
Stack          1    2   16
st             5    9   13   14
st'            5    9   14
```

The cross referencer assumes that its input file is a `.e` file.

A.5   Interface to UNIX

When at the command level, and also when using the interpreter, the user may execute a UNIX command by preceding it with the ! character. For example,

>> !cat myfile.e

sends the command `cat myfile.e` to UNIX from the command level. Similarly,

expr> !cat myfile.e

sends the same command to UNIX from the interpreter. The system handles these commands by creating a sub-shell to execute the command. The sub-shell lasts for the duration of the command. Once the execution is completed, control will be returned back to the origin (i.e., the command level or the interpreter).

One can also create a sub-shell to be used for executing more than one command. To do this one may type ! on its own, e.g.:

>> !
$

The $ sign indicates that we are within a sub-shell. The user may remain in the sub-shell and execute UNIX commands for an arbitrary length of time. To go back, a ^Z (i.e., control Z) must be typed which will terminate the sub-shell and transfer control to the previous level:

$ ^Z
>>

A.5.1   Synopsis and help

The user may obtain assistance on a topic using the synopsis or help command. The synopsis command is ? and gives a brief description of a subject or command. The help command is ?? and gives more detailed explanation. For example,

```
>> ?card
```

or
```
expr> ?card
```

will produce:

```
OPERATOR:      card s
               where s is a set.
```

whereas

```
>> ??card
```
or

```
expr> ??card
```

will produce:

```
OPERATOR:  card s
           where s is a set.
DESCRIP:   Returns the cardinality of s, that is, the number
           of elements of s.
EXAMPLE:   card {2,5,3} = 3
```

The synopsis or help command on its own describes the facility itself, e.g.:

```
>> ?
COMMAND:  ? subject
DESCRIP:  This is the synopsis command. It gives brief
          description on a subject.
>>
```

A.5.2   The executer

The executer is a compact program intended for running complete systems. This program is separate from the rest of the environment and, therefore, runs independently. To run it at UNIX shell level one should type

```
$ epx mysystem
```

where $ is the UNIX prompt and mysystem is the system to be executed. The executer assumes that its input is a .l or .o file. If both exist the .o file will be assumed, unless the full file name is typed.

It is important to note that the executer can only run complete systems. When invoked, it first loads the given system and then automatically executes its design body. If the system is incomplete (i.e., there is no design body) it will terminate immediately. If no system name is specified it will produce the following message and terminate.

```
epx: no source file?
```

To invoke the executer from within EPROS the ! command must be used, e.g.:

```
>> !epx mysystem
```

A.5.3 File conventions

The naming of files in EPROS follows the conventions described below. Each file ends with a period symbol and a letter. The letter signifies the type of the file:

.e source file (i.e., EPROL file)
.l intermediate file (i.e., LISP file)
.o object file (i.e., machine code)
.m module file (i.e., for separate compilation)
.x cross reference file
.t compiler source listing file

When using the tools, the file endings may be dropped. The tools will automatically assume the correct ending.

Appendix B
The Library System

B.1 User interface specification

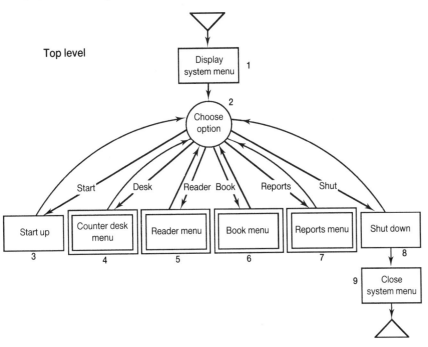

Top level

Counter desk menu

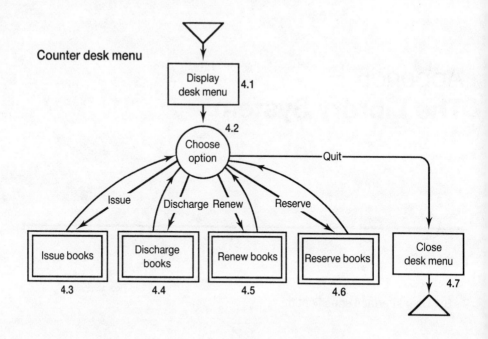

Reader menu

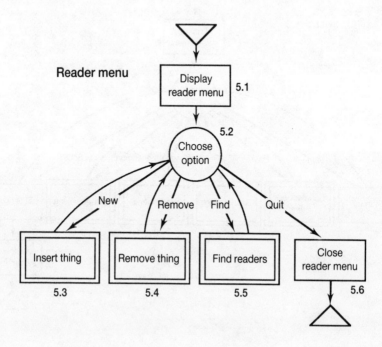

Book menu

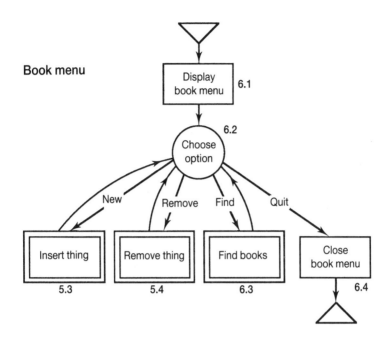

Reports menu

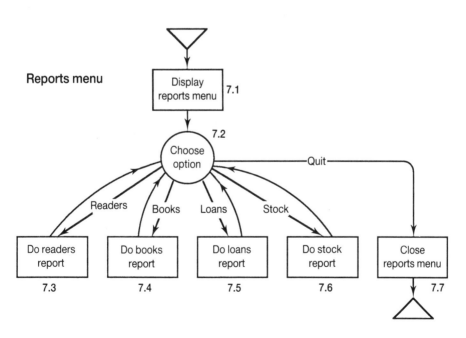

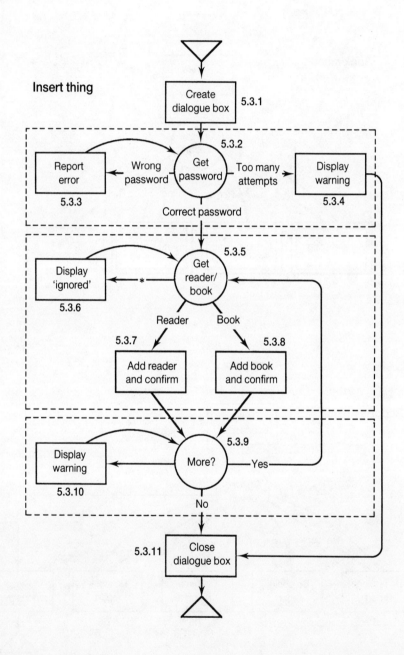

Remove thing

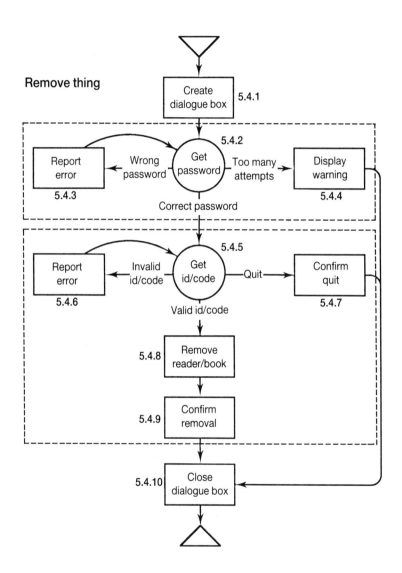

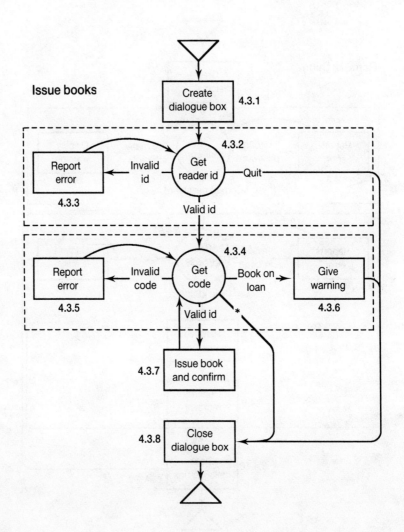

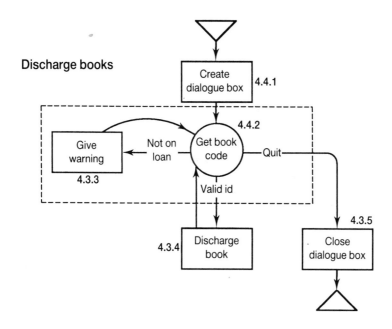

Discharge books

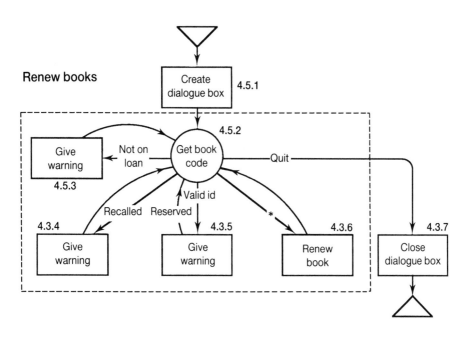

Renew books

Reserve books

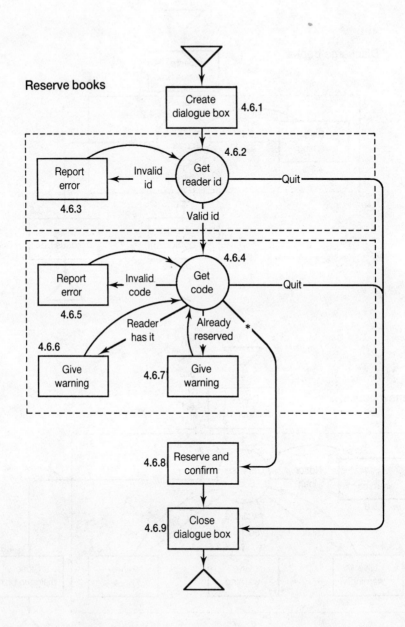

Find readers

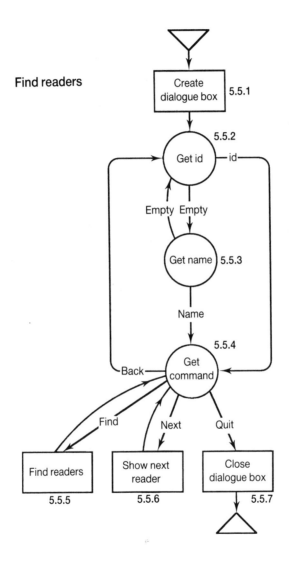

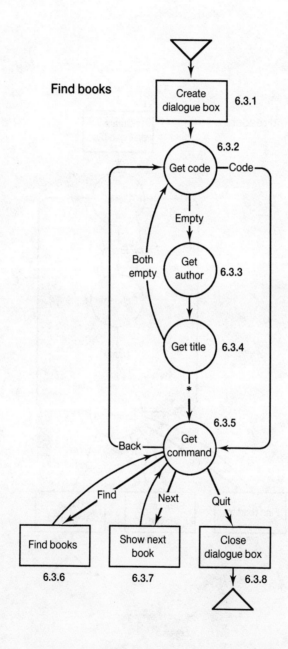

Find books

B.2 Final prototype

```
%library "scr"           /* screen management library */
%library "str"           /* string library */
%library "io"            /* IO library */
%library "dbase"         /* database library */

CONST MONTHS = <"Jan","Feb","Mar","Apr","May","Jun",
                "Jul","Aug","Sep","Oct","Nov","Dec">;
      DEL_PASS    = "r2d2";
      INS_PASS    = "x2y2";
      ATTEMPT_LIM = 3;
      READER = 'R';
      BOOK   = 'B';
      NOTE   = 'N';
      WARN   = 'W';

DOM Id       = Nat0;
    Code     = Nat0;
    Author   = Str;
    Title    = Str;
    Date     = Nat;
    Day_no   = Nat;
    Recall   = {0:4};
    Name     = Str;
    Position = Nat0;
    What     = {READER,BOOK};
    Message  = {NOTE,WARN};

DESIGN library_system();
DOM Reader :: id:    Id,
              pos:   Position,
              name:  Name,
              valid: Bool,
              count: Nat0,
              loan:  Code-list;

    Book ::   code: Code,
              pos:  Position,
              auth: Author,
              titl: Title;

    Loan ::   code: Code,
              rd:   [Id],
```

```
                    date: Date,
                    rec:  Recall,
                    res:  Reserve-list;

        Reserve :: date: Date,
                   rd:   Id,
                   till: [Date];

        TopDate :: no: Nat, y:  Nat, m: Nat, d: Nat;
        ReadersDb = Reader-dbase(key = id);
        BooksDb   = Book-dbase(key = code);
        LoansDb   = Loan-dbase(key = code);
        ReaderForm = form ReaderReg;
        BookForm   = form BookRec;

VAR rds_db: ReadersDb;
    bks_db: BooksDb;
    lns_db: LoansDb;
    rds_list: Reader-list := <>;
    bks_list: Book-list   := <>;
    new_rds: ReaderForm-list := <>;
    rmv_rds: Id-list         := <>;
    new_bks: BookForm-list    := <>;
    rmv_bks: Bool := TRUE;
    ins_ok:  Bool := TRUE;
    del_ok:  Bool := TRUE;
    started: Bool := FALSE;
    stock_rep_ready: Bool := FALSE;
    day_no:   Nat;
    cur_date: TopDate;

FORM ReaderReg
  \
                                        Date:  $date
        Surname:   $sname              Title: $title
        Forenames: $fname1      $fname2
        Position:  $pos
        Faculty:   $fac          Extension: $ext
        Home Address: $road
                      $town
                      $pcode
        Telephone No: $telno     Leaving date: $d/$m/$y \

    $date:   Str(8), system(sdate);
    $sname:  Str(20);
```

```
  $title:  Str(4);
  $fname1: Str(15);
  $fname2: Str(15), optional;
  $pos:    Str(2), computed menu {
                  "^M Position ^N"
                  "Dean"                  → {$pos := "DN"; exit};
                  "Senior Lecturer"       → {$pos := "SL"; exit};
                  "Lecturer"              → {$pos := "LC"; exit};
                  "Visitor"               → {$pos := "VS"; exit};
                  "Research Fellow"       → {$pos := "RF"; exit};
                  "Research Assistant"    → {$pos := "RA"; exit};
                  "Research Student"      → {$pos := "RS"; exit};
                  "Technician"            → {$pos := "TC"; exit};
                  "Secretary"             → {$pos := "SC"; exit};
                  };
  $fac:    Str(11), computed menu {
                  "^M Faculty ^N"
                  "Art"                   → {$fac := itself; exit};
                  "Education"             → {$fac := itself; exit};
                  "Geography"             → {$fac := itself; exit};
                  "Mathematics"           → {$fac := itself; exit};
                  "Sciences"              → {$fac := itself; exit};
                  "Technology"            → {$fac := itself; exit};
                  };
  $ext:    Nat(4), constraint 1000 ≤ $ext ≤ 9999;
  $road:   Str(30);
  $town:   Str(30);
  $pcode:  Str(7), optional;
  $telno:  Nat(7), optional;
  $d:      Nat(2), constraint 1 ≤ $d ≤ 31;
  $m:      Nat(2), constraint 1 ≤ $m ≤ 12;
  $y:      Nat(2), constraint time('Y') ≤ $y ≤ 99;
END ReaderReg

FORM BookRec
  \
                                              Date: $edate
    Class:  L$cl.$cr           Purchase Date: $d/$m/$y
    Author: $i. $auth                   Year: $year
    Title:  $titl
    Volume: $vol                     Edition: $edtn
    Publsh: $pub                         ISBN: 0-$s1-$s2  -$s3\

  $edate: Str(8),  system(sdate);
  $cl:    Nat0(3), constraint 0 ≤ $cl ≤ 799;
```

```
$cr:    Nat0(3);
$d:     Nat(2),   constraint 1 ⩽ $d ⩽ 31, initially time('D');
$m:     Nat(2),   constraint 1 ⩽ $m ⩽ 12, initially time('M');
$y:     Nat(2),   initially time('Y');
$i:     Str(2);
$auth:  Str(20);
$year:  Nat(4),   after($y), constraint $year ⩽ 1900 + $y;
$titl:  Str(60);
$vol:   Nat0(2), initially 0;
$edtn:  Nat(2),  initially 1;
$pub:   Str(30), optional;
$s1:    Nat(3);
$s2:    Nat(5);
$s3:    Nat(1);
END BookRec

FUNCTION init_readers();
VAR rdf:     File;
    rds_cnt: Nat0;
    id:      Id;
    pos:     Position := 0;
    valid:   Bool;
    count:   Nat0;
    loan:    Code;
    loans:   Code-list := <>;
    rd_fm:   ReaderForm;
BEGIN
    rdf := f_open("readers","r");
    db_init(rds_db);
    get(rdf,rds_cnt);
    f_zap(rdf);
    for i in {1:rds_cnt} do {
        get(rdf,id,valid,count);
        for j in {1: count} do {
            get(rdf,loan);
            loans := loans ⁀ <loan>;
        };
        fm_get(rdf,rd_fm);
        db_insert(rds_db,
              mk-Reader(id,pos,rd_fm.$sname,valid,count,loans));
        pos := pos+1;
    };
    f_close(rdf);
END init_readers
 FUNCTION init_books();
```

```
VAR bkf:     File;
    bks_cnt: Nat0;
    code:    Code;
    bk_fm:   BookForm;
    pos:     Position := 0;
BEGIN
    bkf := f_open("books","r");
    db_init(bks_db);
    get(bkf,bks_cnt);
    f_zap(bkf);
    for i in {1:bks_cnt} do {
        get(bkf,code);
        fm_get(bkf,bk_fm);
        db_insert(bks_db,
        mk-Book(code,pos,bk_fm.$auth,bk_fm.$titl));
        pos := pos+1;
    };
    f_close(bkf);
END init_books

FUNCTION init_loans (): Day_no;
VAR lnf:     File;
    lns_cnt,rs_cnt: Nat0;
    date,rs_date:   Date;
    rd,rs_rd:       Id;
    code:    Code;
    rec:     Recall;
    rs_till: [Date];
    res:     Reserve-list := <>;
    day_no:  Nat;
BEGIN
    lnf := f_open("loans","r");
    db_init(lns_db);
    get(lnf,lns_cnt,day_no);
    f_zap(lnf);

    for i in {1:lns_cnt} do {
        get(lnf,code,rd,date,rec,rs_cnt);
        for j in {1:rs_cnt} do {
            get(lnf,rs_date,rs_rd,rs_till);
            res := res ~ <mk-Reserve(rs_date,rs_rd,
                    if rs_till = 0 then NIL else rs_till)>;
        };
        db_insert(lns_db,mk-Loan(code,if rd=0 then NIL
                                    else rd,date,rec,res));
```

```
    };
    f_close(lnf);
    return(day_no+1);
END init_loans

FUNCTION is_element_of(obj: Id | Code, objl: (Id | Code)-list):
Bool;
BEGIN
    while objl ≠ <> do {
        if obj = hd objl then
            return(TRUE);
        objl := tl objl;
    };
    return(FALSE);
END is_element_of


FUNCTION is_expired(y: Nat, m: Nat, d: Nat): Bool;
BEGIN
    return(y*365+m*30+d < cur_date.no);
END is_expired


FUNCTION update_readers(rds_db: ReadersDb,
 new_rds: ReaderForm-list, rmv_rds: Id-list);
VAR rdf,logf,tempf:    File;
    valid, stays:      Bool := FALSE;
    rds_cnt, lns_cnt:  Nat0;
    rd_fm:     ReaderForm;
    id :       Id    := 0;
    rds_cnt': Nat0 := 0;
    code:      Code;
    rd:        Reader;
    loans:     Code-list;
    loan:      [Loan];
BEGIN
    rdf := f_open("readers","r");
    logf := f_open("readers.log","w");
    tempf := f_open("temp","w");
    get(rdf,rds_cnt);
    f_zap(rdf);
    put(tempf,"%05d^n",rds_cnt');
    for i in {1:rds_cnt} do {
        get(rdf,id,valid,lns_cnt);
        for j in {1:lns_cnt} do
            get(rdf,code);
        fm_get(rdf,rd_fm);
```

```
rd := db_find(rds_db,id);
loans := rd.loan;
if is_element_of(id,rmv_rds) then {
   put(logf,
      "* Reader Removed: %5d %s Reg. on %02d-%02d-%02d ^n",
         id, rd_fm.$sname, rd_fm.$d, rd_fm.$m, rd_fm.$y);
   while loans ≠ <> do {
     loan := db_find(lns_db,hd loans);
     put(logf,"Lost Book: %06d by %05d ^n",loan.code,id);
     loans := tl loans;
    }
}
else if is_expired(rd_fm.$y,rd_fm.$m,rd_fm.$d) then {
   if (rd.count > 0) then {
      rd.valid := FALSE;
      while loans ≠ <> do {
        loan := db_find(lns_db,hd loans);
        if loan.rec = 0 then {
          loan.rec := 1;
          put(logf,
          "Recall Book: %06d from %05d ^n",loan.code, id);
        };
           loans := tl loans;
        };
        stays := TRUE;
    }
   else
      put(logf,"Reader Removed: %05d %s Reg. on %02d-
      %02d-%02d ^n",id, rd_fm.$sname, rd_fm.$d,
      rd_fm.$m, rd_fm.$y);
}
else
   stays := TRUE;
if stays then {
   put(tempf,"%d %s %d",id,
        if rd.valid then "TRUE" else "FALSE",rd.count);
   loans := rd.loan;
   for i in {1:rd.count} do {
      put(tempf, "%d", hd loans);
      loans := tl loans;
   };
   fm_put(tempf,rd_fm);
   rds_cnt' := rds_cnt'+1;
};
};
```

```
    while new_rds ≠ <> do {
        id := id + 1;
        rd_fm := hd new_rds;
        put(tempf,"%d %s %d",id,"TRUE",0);
        fm_put(tempf,rd_fm);
        put(logf,"New Reader: %5d %20s on %d-%d-%d^n",
                id, rd_fm.$sname, rd_fm.$d, rd_fm.$m, rd_fm.$d);
        rds_cnt' := rds_cnt'+1;
        new_rds := tl new_rds;
    };
    f_close(rdf);
    f_close(tempf);
    f_close(logf);
    tempf := f_open("temp","r+w");
    put(tempf,"%05d^n",rds_cnt');
    f_close(tempf);
    f_copy("temp","readers");
END update_readers

FUNCTION update_books(new_bks: BookForm-list, rmv_bks: Code-
list);
VAR bkf,logf,tempf: File;
    bk_fm:     BookForm;
    id:        Id;
    code :     Code := 0;
    pos  :     Position;
    stays:     Bool := FALSE;
    bks_cnt:   Int;
    bks_cnt':  Int := 0;
    bk:        Book;
BEGIN
    bkf := f_open("books","r");
    logf := f_open("books.log","w");
    tempf := f_open("temp","w");
    get(bkf,bks_cnt);
    f_zap(bkf);
    put(tempf,"%05d^n",bks_cnt');
    for i in {1:bks_cnt} do {
        get(bkf,code);
        fm_get(bkf,bk_fm);
        if is_element_of(id,rmv_bks) then
            put(logf,
                "Book Removed: %06d %s-%4d Purch. on %02d-%02d-%02d
                ^n",code,bk_fm.$auth,bk_fm.$year,bk_fm.$d,bk_fm.$m,
```

```
            bk_fm.$y)
        else {
            put(tempf,"%d",code);
            fm_put(tempf,bk_fm);
            bks_cnt' := bks_cnt'+1;
        };
    };
    while new_bks ≠ <> do {
        code := code + 1;
        bk_fm:= hd new_bks;
        put(tempf,"%d",code);
        fm_put(tempf,bk_fm);
        put(logf,"New Book: %06d %s/%4d on %02d-%02d-%02d ^n",
        code,bk_fm.$auth,bk_fm.$year,bk_fm.$d,bk_fm.$m,bk_fm.$d);
        bks_cnt' := bks_cnt'+1;
        new_bks := tl new_bks;
    };
    f_close(bkf);
    f_close(tempf);
    f_close(logf);
    tempf := f_open("temp","r+w");
    put(tempf,"%05d^n",bks_cnt');
    f_close(tempf);
    f_copy("temp","books");
END update_books

FUNCTION update_loans (lns_db: LoansDb, rds_db: ReadersDb, VAR
rmv_rds: Id-list);
VAR lnf,logf: File;
    lns_list: Loan-list := db_list(lns_db);
    rds_list: Reader-list := db_list(rds_db);
    lns_cnt: Nat0 := len lns_list;
    loan:    Loan;
    ln:      Code-list;
    resl:    Reserve-list;
    res:     Reserve;
    lost:    Code-list := <>;
    reader:  Reader;
    stays:   Bool := TRUE;
BEGIN
    lnf := f_open("loans","w");
    logf := f_open("loans.log","w");
    put(lnf,"%d %d^n",lns_cnt,day_no);
    while lns_list ≠ <> do {
        loan := hd lns_list;
```

```
resl := loan.res;
if loan.rec = 0 then {
    if loan.rd = NIL then {
        if resl = <> then
            stays := FALSE
        else if resl[1].till ≠ NIL ∧
                resl[1].till < cur_date.no then {
            loan.res := tl resl;
            if loan.res = <> then
                stays := FALSE
            else {
                loan.res[1].till := cur_date.no + 14;
                put(logf,"Reserved: %06d for %05d^n",
                        loan.code,loan.res[1].rd);
            };
        }
        else
            stays := FALSE;
    }
    else if loan.date+14 > cur_date.no then {
        loan.rec := 1;
        put(logf,"Recall Book: %06d from %05d ^n",
                loan.code,loan.rd);
    }
}
else if loan.rd = NIL then
    stays := FALSE
else if loan.rec<4 ∧
        loan.rec*30+14 ≤ cur_date.no - loan.date then {
    loan.rec := loan.rec+1;
    put(logf,"Recall Book(%d): %06d from %05d^n",
            loan.rec,loan.code,loan.rd);
}
else if loan.rec = 4 ∧ loan.rec*30+14 > 200 then
    lost := <loan.code> ~ lost;
if stays then {
    put(lnf,"%d %d %d %d %d ",
    loan.code, loan.rd, loan.date, loan.rec, len resl);
    while resl ≠ <> do {
        res := hd resl;
        put(lnf,"%d %d %d ", res.date, res.rd,
                if res.till = NIL then 0 else
                res.till);
        resl := tl resl;
    };
```

```
                put(lnf,"^n");
            };
            lns_list := tl lns_list;
        };
    while rds_list ≠ <> do {
        reader := hd rds_list;
        ln := reader.loan;
        while ln ≠ <> do {
            if ¬is_element_of(hd ln,lost) then
                done;
            ln := tl ln;
        };
        if reader.loan ≠ <> ∧ ln ≠ <> then
            rmv_rds := rmv_rds ⌢ <reader.id>;
        rds_list := tl rds_list;
    };
    f_close(lnf);
    f_close(logf);
END update_loans
```

```
FUNCTION is_reserved_for(id: Id, resl: Reserve-list): Bool;
BEGIN
    while resl ≠ <> do {
        if id = (hd resl).rd then
            return(TRUE);
        resl := tl resl;
    };
    return(FALSE);
END is_reserved_for
```

```
FUNCTION message(line: Nat, kind: Message, message: Str);
BEGIN
    if kind = WARN then
        bell();
    w_move(line,2);
    w_put("^R%s",message);
    for i in {1 : w_spec('C') - st_len(message) - 2} do
        w_put(" ");
    w_put("^N");
END message
```

```
DIALOGUE remove_thing(what: What,
VAR rmv_list: (Id | Code)-list, VAR del_ok: Bool);
VAR width:    Nat := 30;
```

```
        passwd:    Str;
        attempts:  Nat0 := 0;
        ic:        Id | Code;
BEGIN
    state box: { assert(del_ok);
                 w_open(3,width, if what = READER then
                                        "^M Remove Reader ^N"
                                 else "^M Remove Book ^N");
                 message(3,NOTE,"");
               }                                    → pass;

    iap pass: { w_move(1,1);
                w_get(" Password:  ",passwd,8,noecho);
                message(3,NOTE,"");
              };
            : passwd = DEL_PASS                      → read;
            : attempts ⩾ ATTEMPT_LIM,
              { message(3,WARN,"Imposter!");
                wait(2);
                del_ok := FALSE;
              }                                      → out;
            : TRUE, { attempts := attempts+1;
                      message(3,WARN,"Wrong!");
                    }                                → pass;

    iap read: { w_move(2,1);
                if what = READER then
                    w_get(" Reader Id: ",ic,5)
                else
                    w_get(" Book Code: ",ic,6);
              };
            : (if what = READER then db_find(rds_db,ic)
               else db_find(bks_db,ic)) ≠ NIL,
              { rmv_list := rmv_list ~ <ic>;
                message(3,NOTE,"Ok");
              }                                              → out;
            : ic = 0, message(3,NOTE,"Quited")               → out;
            : TRUE,   message(3,WARN,"Non-existant!")         → read;

    state out: w_close(1)  → return;
END remove_thing

DIALOGUE insert_thing(what: What,
                      VAR new_list:(ReaderForm | BookForm)-list,
                      VAR ins_ok: Bool);
```

```
VAR width:     Nat := 30;
    passwd:    Str;
    attempts:  Nat0 := 0;
    ok:        Bool;
    resp:      Char;
    rd_fm:     ReaderForm;
    bk_fm:     BookForm;
BEGIN
    state  box: { assert(ins_ok);
                  w_open(3,width, if what = READER
                                  then "^M New Reader ^N"
                                  else "^M New Book ^N");
                  message(3,NOTE,"");
                }                              → pass;

    iap   pass: { w_move(1,1);
                  w_get(" Password:    ",passwd,8,noecho);
                  message(3,NOTE,"");
                };
               : passwd = INS_PASS              → read;
               : attempts ⩾ ATTEMPT_LIM,
                 { message(3,WARN,"Imposter!");
                   wait(2);
                   ins_ok := FALSE;
                 }                              → out;
               : TRUE, { attempts := attempts+1;
                         message(3,WARN,"Wrong!");
                       }                        → pass;

    iap read: ok := if what = READER then
                        fm_new(rd_fm,"^M New Reader ^N")
                    else
                        fm_new(bk_fm,"^M New Book ^N");
            : ok ∧ what = READER,
              { new_list := new_list ⁀ <rd_fm>;
                message(3,NOTE,"Registered");
              }                                 → next;
            : ok ∧ what = BOOK,
              { new_list := new_list ⁀ <bk_fm>;
                message(3,NOTE,"Recorded");
              }                                 → next;
            : TRUE, message(3,NOTE,"Ignored")   → next;

    iap next: { w_move(2,1);
                w_put(" More [y/n]:       ");
```

```
                        w_move(2,14);
                        resp := keybd();
                      };
                    : resp = 'y' ∨ resp = 'Y', w_put("yes")      → read;
                    : resp = 'n' ∨ resp = 'N', w_put("no ")      → out;
                    : TRUE, message(3,WARN,"Yes or No please")   → next;
        state out: w_close(1)                                    → return;
END insert_thing


DIALOGUE issue_books (rds_db: ReadersDb, bks_db: BooksDb,
                        lns_db: LoansDb);
VAR width: Nat := 30;
    id:    Id;
    code:  Code;
BEGIN
    state box: { w_open(3,width,"^M Issue ^N");
                  message(3,NOTE,"");
                }                              → reader;

    iap reader: { w_move(1,1);
                    w_get(" Reader Id: ",id,5);
                  };
                  : id = 0                                     → out;
                  : db_find(rds_db,id) = NIL,
                    message(3,WARN,"No such reader")   → reader;
                  : TRUE                                       → book;

    iap book: { w_move(2,1);
                  w_get(" Book Code: ",code,6);
                };
                : code = 0                                     → out;
                : db_find(bks_db,code) = NIL,
                  message(3,WARN,"No such book")     → book;
                : db_find(lns_db,code) ≠ NIL,
                  message(3,WARN,"Is on loan")       → book;
                : TRUE                                         → issue;

    state issue: { db_insert(lns_db,
                    mk-Loan(code,id,cur_date.no,0,<>));
                      message(3,NOTE,"Issued");
                  }                            → book;

    state out: w_close(1)                                     → return;
END issue_books
```

```
FUNCTION del_element(code: Code, codel: Code-list);
VAR head: Code := hd codel;
    tail: Code-list := tl codel;
    idx:  Nat := 2;
BEGIN
    if code ≠ head then
        while tail ≠ <> do {
            if code = hd tail then {
                codel[idx] := head;
                codel := tl codel;
                done;
            };
            tail := tl tail;
            idx := idx+1;
        }
    else
        codel := tl codel;
END del_element


DIALOGUE discharge_books(rds_db: ReadersDb, lns_db: LoansDb);
VAR width: Nat := 30;
    code:   Code;
    loan:   [Loan];
    reader: Reader;
BEGIN
    state box: { w_open(3,width,"^M Discharge ^N");
                 message(2,NOTE,"");
                 message(3,NOTE,"");
               }                               → book;

    iap book: { w_move(1,1);
                w_get(" Book Code: ",code,6);
              };
            :code = 0                          → out;
            :(loan := db_find(lns_db,code)) = NIL ∨
                                          loan.rd = NIL,
              message(2,WARN,"Is not on loan") → book;
            : TRUE                             → disch;

    state disch: { reader := db_find(rds_db,loan.rd);
                   del_element(code,reader.loan);
                   loan.rd := NIL;
                   message(2,NOTE,"Discharged");
                   mac {
```

```
                      loan.rec>0   → message(3,WARN,
                                         "Goes to RECALLED shelf");
                      loan.res=<>  → { message(3,NOTE,
                                            "Goes to shelves");
                                       db_delete(lns_db,code);
                                     };
                      TRUE         → { message(3,WARN,
                                            "Goes to RESERVE shelf");
                                       loan.res[1].till := cur_date.no;
                                     };
                    };
                  }                                   → book;
        state out: w_close(1)                         → return;
END discharge_books


DIALOGUE renew_books(lns_db: LoansDb);
VAR width:  Nat := 30;
    code:   Code;
    loan:   [Loan];
    reader: Reader;
BEGIN
    state box: { w_open(2,width,"^M Renew ^N");
                 message(2,NOTE,"");
               }                                       → book;

    iap book: { w_move(1,1);
                w_get(" Book Code: ",code,6);
              };
            : code = 0                                 → out;
            :(loan := db_find(lns_db,code))=NIL ∨ loan.rd = NIL,
              message(2,WARN,"Is not on loan")         → book;
            : loan.rec > 0,
              message(2,WARN,"Recalled - can't renew") → book;
            : loan.res ≠ <>,
              message(2,WARN,"Reserved - can't renew") → book;
            : TRUE                                     → renew;

    state renew: loan.date := cur_date.no             → out;
    state out: w_close(1)                             → return;
END renew_books


DIALOGUE reserve_books(rds_db: ReadersDb, lns_db: LoansDb);
VAR width: Nat := 30;
    id:    Id;
    code:  Code;
```

```
    loan:  [Loan];
BEGIN
    state box:  { w_open(3,width,"^M Reserve ^N");
                  message(3,NOTE,"");
                }                          → reader;
    iap reader:  { w_move(1,1);
                   w_get(" Reader Id: ",id,5);
                 };
                 : id = 0                               → out;
                 : db_find(rds_db,id) = NIL,
                   message(3,WARN,"No such reader")  → reader;
                 : TRUE                               → book;

    iap book:  { w_move(2,1);
                 w_get(" Book Code: ",code,6);
               };
               : code = 0                              → out;
               : (loan := db_find(lns_db,code)) = NIL,
                 message(3,WARN,"Is not on loan")           → book;
               : loan.rd = id,
                 message(3,WARN,"Reader has the book")       → book;
               : is_reserved_for(id,loan.res),
                 message(3,WARN,"Already reserved for reader")→ book;
               : TRUE                                → reserve;

    state reserve:  { loan.res := loan.res ~ <mk-
                        Reserve(cur_date.no,id,NIL)>;
                      message(3,NOTE,"Reserved");
                    }                          → book;
    state out: w_close(1)                      → return;
END reserve_books

CLUSTER dial_box {
            title:Const: Str
            { 'field' fld:Const: Str ','
                    fid:Ident: (Str | Int | Real)
                    ':' fsz:Const: Nat
                    ',' 'empty' emp:Const: (Str | Int | Real)
                    [ '→' 'commands']co ';'
            }+fr
            { 'command' comnd:Const: Str '→' action:Statm
                                        ['→' 'fields']fo ';'
            }+cr
          };
VAR flen: Nat0;
```

```
      lins: Nat := fr+3;
      cols: Nat;
      sum:  Nat := 2;
      max_len, max_siz: Nat := 1;
      com_pos: array[cr+1] Nat;
      id:   Str | Int | Real;
      ch:   Char;
      op:   Nat;
BEGIN
    for i in {1:fr} do {
        if (flen := st_len(fld[i])) > max_len then
          max_len := flen;
        if fsz[i] > max_siz then
          max_siz := fsz[i];
    };
    cols := max_len+max_siz;
    for i in {1:cr} do {
        com_pos[i] := sum;
        sum := com_pos[i]+st_len(comnd[i])+2;
    };
    if sum > cols then
      cols := sum;

    w_open(lins,cols,title);
    for i in {1:fr} do
        w_put("%s^n",fld[i]);
    for i in {1:cr} do {
        w_move(fr+1,com_pos[i]+1);
        w_put("^R%s^N",comnd[i]);
    };
    message(lins,NOTE,"");

    while TRUE do {
        for i in {1:fr} do {
            w_move(i,max_len+1);
            w_get(id,fsz[i]);
            fid[i] := id;
            if fid[i] ≠ emp[i] ∧ co[i] = 1 then
                done;
        };
        op := 1;
        while TRUE do {
            w_move(fr+1,com_pos[op]+1);
            w_put("^M%s^N",comnd[op]);
            w_move(fr+1,com_pos[op]);
```

```
            cases (ch := keybd()) {
              'F1' → { w_put(" ^R%s^N",comnd[op]);
                       op := if op = 1 then cr else op-1;
                     };
              'F2' → { w_put(" ^R%s^N",comnd[op]);
                       op := if op = cr then 1 else op+1;
                     };
              '^r' → { action[op];
                       if fo[op] = 1 then {
                           w_put(" ^R%s^N",comnd[op]);
                           done;
                       };
                     };
              TRUE → bell();
            };
        };
    };
     on_exit do
       w_close(1);
END dial_box



FUNCTION sort_by_pos(items: (Reader | Book)-list);
VAR swap:   Bool := TRUE;
    length: Nat0 := len items;
    temp:   (Reader | Book);
BEGIN
    while swap do {
        swap := FALSE;
        for i in {1:length-1} do
            if items[i].pos > items[i+1].pos then {
                temp := items[i];
                items[i] := items[i+1];
                items[i+1] := temp;
                swap := TRUE;
            };
    };
END sort_by_pos



FUNCTION find_readers_dial(rds_db: ReadersDb);
VAR id:      Id;
    sname:   Name;
    readers: ReaderForm-list := <>;
    count:   Nat0 := 0;
```

```
FUNCTION find_readers(id: Id, sname: Name): ReaderForm-
                                                 list;
VAR rdf:        File;
    rds_cnt:    Nat0;
    rd:         [Reader];
    rds_list':  Reader-list;
    rds:        Reader-list := <>;
    rd_fm:      ReaderForm;
    rd_fms:     ReaderForm-list := <>;
    valid:      Bool;
    count:      Nat0;
    code:       Code;
    from:       Position;

BEGIN
    rdf := f_open("readers","r");
    get(rdf,rds_cnt);
    f_zap(rdf);
    if id ≠ 0 then {
       if (rd := db_find(rds_db,id)) ≠ NIL then {
          for i in {1:rd.pos} do
              f_zap(rdf);
          get(rdf,id,valid,count);
          for i in {1:count} do
              get(rdf,code);
          fm_get(rdf,rd_fm);
          f_close(rdf);
          rd_fms := <rd_fm>;
       };
    }
    else {
       rds_list' := rds_list;
       while rds_list' ≠ <> do {
             if st_sub(sname,(hd rds_list').name) then
                rds := rds ⌢ <hd rds_list'>;
             rds_list' := tl rds_list';
       };
       if rds ≠ <> then {
          sort_by_pos(rds);
          from := 0;
          while rds ≠ <> do {
              for i in {from:(hd rds).pos-1} do
                  f_zap(rdf);
              get(rdf,id,valid,count);
              for i in {1:count} do
```

```
                        get(rdf,code);
                    fm_get(rdf,rd_fm);
                    rd_fms := rd_fms ^ <rd_fm>;
                    from := (hd rds).pos+1;
                    rds := tl rds;
                };
            };
        };
        f_close(rdf);
        return(rd_fms);
    END find_readers

BEGIN
    dial_box {
        "^M Find Reader ^N"
        field " Id Number: ",  id: 5,  empty 0 → commands;
        field " Surname: ", sname: 20, empty "" ;
        command " FIND " → {
                readers := find_readers(id,sname);
                count := 1;
                cases len readers {
                  0    → message(5,WARN,"Can't find reader");
                  1    → fm_view(hd readers,"");
                  TRUE → message(5,NOTE,st_app(st_num(len
                            readers)," hits"));
                };
        };
        command " NEXT " → {
                if readers = <> then
                    message(5,WARN,"No reader found yet")
                else {
                    fm_view(hd readers,st_app(st_app("^M Item ⇒",
                                                    st_num(count)),
                                         " ^N"));
                    count := count+1;
                    readers := tl readers;
                    message(5,NOTE,st_app(st_num(len readers),
                                        " remaining"));
                };
        };
        command " BACK " → message(5,NOTE,"") → fields;
        command " QUIT " → exit;
    };
END find_readers_dial
```

```
FUNCTION find_books_dial(bks_db: BooksDb);
VAR code:  Code;
    auth:  Author;
    title: Title;
    books: BookForm-list;
    count: Nat0 := 0;

    FUNCTION find_books(code: Id, auth: Author, title: Title):
                        BookForm-list;
    VAR bkf:       File;
        rds_cnt:   Nat0;
        bk:        [Book];
        bks_list': Book-list;
        bks:       Book-list := <>;
        bk_fm:     BookForm;
        bk_fms:    BookForm-list := <>;
        from:      Position;
    BEGIN
        bkf := f_open("books","r");
        get(bkf,rds_cnt);
        f_zap(bkf);
        if code + 0 then {
            if (bk := db_find(bks_db,code)) + NIL then {
                for i in {1:bk.pos} do
                    f_zap(bkf);
                get(bkf,code);
                fm_get(bkf,bk_fm);
                f_close(bkf);
                bk_fms := <bk_fm>;
            };
        }
        else {
            bks_list' := bks_list;
            while bks_list' + <> do {
                if st_sub(auth,(hd bks_list').auth) ∧
                    st_sub(title,(hd bks_list').titl) then
                    bks := bks ⌢ <hd bks_list'>;
                bks_list' := tl bks_list';
            };
            if bks + <> then {
                sort_by_pos(bks);
                from := 0;
                while bks + <> do {
                    for i in {from:(hd bks).pos-1} do
```

```
                    f_zap(bkf);
                get(bkf,code);
                fm_get(bkf,bk_fm);
                bk_fms := bk_fms ~ <bk_fm>;
                from := (hd bks).pos+1;
                bks := tl bks;
            };
          };
        };
        f_close(bkf);
        return(bk_fms);
    END find_books
BEGIN
    dial_box {
        "^M Find Book ^N"
        field " Code: ",    code: 6,   empty 0 → commands;
        field " Author: ",  auth: 20, empty "";
        field " Title: ",  title: 25, empty "";
        command " FIND " → {
            books := find_books(code,auth,title);
            count := 1;
            cases len books {
                0    → message(6,WARN,"Can't find book");
                1    → fm_view(hd books,"");
                TRUE → message(6,NOTE,st_app(st_num(len books),
                                                " hits"));
            };
        };
        command " NEXT " → {
            if books = <> then
                message(6,WARN,"No book found yet")
            else {
                fm_view(hd books,st_app(st_app("^M Item ⇒",
                                                st_num(count)),
                                    " ^N"));
                count := count+1;
                books := tl books;
                message(6,NOTE,st_app
                        (st_num(len books),"remaining"));
            };
        };
        command " BACK " → message(6,NOTE,"") → fields;
        command " QUIT " → exit;
    };
END find_books_dial
```

```
FUNCTION start_up ();
BEGIN
    move(24,2);
    put("^MPlease Wait^N");
    init_readers();
    init_books();
    rds_list := db_list(rds_db);
    bks_list := db_list(bks_db);
    day_no := init_loans();
    cur_date := mk-TopDate(0,time('Y'),time('M'),time('D'));
    cur_date.no := cur_date.y*365 + cur_date.m*30 + cur_date.d;
    move(24,2);
    put("^RDAY: %d      ^N",day_no);
    move(24,48);
    put("^RUP: at %02d:%02d:%02d, on %02d %3s %4d",
        time('h'),time('m'),time('s'),
        cur_date.d,MONTHS[cur_date.m],1900+cur_date.y);
END start_up


FUNCTION counter_desk_menu ();
BEGIN
    menu {
        "^M Counter Desk ^N"
        "Issue"      → issue_books(rds_db,bks_db,lns_db);
        "Discharge"  → discharge_books(rds_db,lns_db);
        "Renew"      → renew_books(lns_db);
        "Reserve"    → reserve_books(rds_db,lns_db);
        "Quit"       → exit;
        TRUE         → exit;
    };
END counter_desk_menu


FUNCTION reader_menu ();
BEGIN
    menu {
        "^M Reader ^N"
        "New Reader",    constraint ins_ok →
                         insert_thing(READER,new_rds,ins_ok);
        "Remove Reader", constraint del_ok →
                         remove_thing(READER,rmv_rds,del_ok);
        "Find Reader"                → find_readers_dial(rds_db);
        "Quit"                       → exit;
        TRUE                         → exit;
    };
END reader_menu
```

```
FUNCTION book_menu ();
BEGIN
    menu {
        "^M Book ^N"
        "New Book",      constraint ins_ok →
                         insert_thing(BOOK,new_bks,ins_ok);
        "Remove Book",   constraint del_ok →
                         remove_thing(BOOK,rmv_bks,del_ok);
        "Find Book"                        →
                          find_books_dial(bks_db);
        "Quit"                             → exit;
        TRUE                               → exit;
    };
END book_menu

FUNCTION report_menu ();
    FUNCTION prepare_stock_report ();
    VAR bkf, stkf: File;
        bks_cnt:   Nat0;
        code:      Code;
        bk_fm:     BookForm;
    BEGIN
        bkf := f_open("books","r");
        stkf := f_open("stock.log","w");
        get(bkf,bks_cnt);
        f_zap(bkf);
        for i in {1:bks_cnt} do {
            get(bkf,code);
            fm_get(bkf,bk_fm);
            put(stkf,
              "%06d %s %s --- L%03d.%03d /%d/ ISBN 0-%03d-%05d-%d
              ^n",code, bk_fm.$auth, bk_fm.$i, bk_fm.$cl,
              bk_fm.$cr,bk_fm.$year, bk_fm.$s1, bk_fm.$s2,
              bk_fm.$s3);
            put(stkf, "        %s ^n        %s, %02d-%02d-%02d --
                  %d(%d) ^n", bk_fm.$titl, bk_fm.$pub, bk_fm.$d,
                  bk_fm.$m, bk_fm.$y,bk_fm.$vol, bk_fm.$edtn);
        };
        f_close(bkf);
        f_close(stkf);
    END prepare_stock_report
BEGIN
    menu {
        "^M Reports ^N"
        "Readers" → w_text(10,60,"^M Readers Log
```

```
                         ^N","readers.log");
     "Books"    → w_text(10,60,"^M Books Log ^N","books.log");
     "Loans"    → w_text(10,60,"^M Loans Log ^N","loans.log");
     "Entire Stock"
                  → { if ¬stock_rep_ready then {
                          w_open(2,27,"");
                          w_put("^BPlease Wait^N...");
                          prepare_stock_report();
                          stock_rep_ready := TRUE;
                          w_close(1);
                       };
                       w_text(10,60,"^M Stock Log
                              ^N","stock.log");
                    };
     "Quit"    → exit;
     TRUE      → exit;
   };
END report_menu

FUNCTION shut_down (started: Bool);
BEGIN
    if started then {
        move(24,2);
        put("^MPlease Wait^N");
        update_loans(lns_db,rds_db,rmv_rds);
        update_readers(rds_db,new_rds,rmv_rds);
        update_books(new_bks,rmv_bks);
    };
END shut_down

BEGIN /* design */
    init_scr();
    put("^R%26sL I B R A R Y    S Y S T E M%26s^N","","");
    move(24,1);
    put("^R%80s^N","");
    move(3,2);

    menu {
       ""
       "Start Up", constraint ¬started →
                                 {start_up(); started := TRUE};
       "Counter Desk", constraint  started →
                                   counter_desk_menu();
       "Reader",       constraint  started → reader_menu();
       "Book",         constraint  started → book_menu();
```

```
        "Reports",        constraint  started → report_menu();
        "Shut Down"  → { shut_down(started); exit; };
    };
    tini_scr();
END library_system
```

Index